MW01196508

LUCKNOW
1857

INDIA'S HISTORIC BATTLES:

A SERIES

LUCKNOW 1857

ROSIE LLEWELLYN-JONES

SERIES EDITED BY

SQN LDR RANA CHHINA (RETD)

HarperCollins *Publishers* India

First published in India by HarperCollins *Publishers* 2022
Building No. 10, Tower A, 4th Floor, DLF Cyber City, Phase II,
Gurugram – 122002
www.harpercollins.co.in

In collaboration with the United Service Institution of India

2 4 6 8 10 9 7 5 3 1

Copyright © Rosie Llewellyn-Jones 2022
Contributing photographer: Anil Mehrotra

P-ISBN: 978-93-5489-405-3
E-ISBN: 978-93-5489-410-7

The views and opinions expressed in this book are the author's own. The facts are
as reported by her and the publishers are not in any way liable for the same.

Rosie Llewellyn-Jones asserts the moral right
to be identified as the author of this work.

All rights reserved. No part of this publication may be reproduced,
stored in a retrieval system, or transmitted, in any form or by any
means, electronic, mechanical, photocopying, recording or otherwise,
without the prior permission of the publishers.

Cover design: Saurav Das
Cover illustration: Mohit Suneja

Typeset in 11.5/15.5 Adobe Garamond at
Manipal Technologies Limited, Manipal

Printed and bound at
Nutech Print Services - India

HarperCollinsIn

This book is produced from independently certified FSC® paper to ensure
responsible forest management.

Contents

'Map of Oudh'. Edinburgh and London: W. & A.K. Johnston.
Scale 64 miles to 1½ inches. Map size 7¼ x 6¼ inches.

Series Editor's Note

WARS AND CONQUESTS HAVE FORMED an integral part of India's history since times immemorial. The country is littered with the ruins of empires that dot the geographical map of the subcontinent along with the sites of battles that mark their passing. Yet, the inexorable advance of 'civilization' and accompanying human pressures on the land have led to the gradual obliteration of a large number of these historic landmarks. In my own lifetime, I have seen landscapes change beyond recognition and watched visible markers of periods past get subsumed by unplanned settlements and urban expansion.

This series on India's Historic Battles stems from a desire to better acquaint people with the rich tapestry of India's military history and to generate an awareness of the physical spaces linked to it. The contributing authors have been chosen as much for their passion as their knowledge of the subjects on which they write. While academic rigour has been applied to the research, the tone of the volumes is not academic. On the contrary, it is intended to appeal to the lay reader, while meeting the requirements of the discerning historian as well. In order to do this, each volume follows a common template— an important part of which is the section that provides practical information for visitors who may intend to 'walk the ground' and see for themselves the physical remains of monuments and spaces that were witness to the events described within their pages.

The series will initially cover the sites of the 1857 Uprising in Awadh, Delhi and Meerut, the First Anglo-Sikh war and the epic

Second World War battles of Kohima and Imphal in Northeast India. It is hoped that the series will provide a fillip to 'battlefield tourism' in the country since each volume can function as a stand-alone battlefield guide that will enable the visitor to gain a better understanding of the historical context of important events. It will hopefully also have the effect of generating awareness about the significance of lesser-known historical spaces and monuments, and thereby contribute to their preservation in the long term.

Sqn Ldr Rana Chhina (Retd)
New Delhi, February 2022

Preface

THE CITY OF LUCKNOW, SITUATED 250 miles south-east of Delhi, was the epicentre of revolt and the most bitterly contested site during the Uprising of 1857 and 1858. The prolonged siege of the British Residency, its eventual relief and the recapture of the city is one of the great epics of nineteenth-century history. It produced some of the most famous characters of the Uprising, including Begam Hazrat Mahal, a divorced queen with a teenage son who became king for a season, and the charismatic but quarrelsome Maulvi Ahmadullah Shah.

Among the British were Brigadier General Sir Henry Lawrence, newly appointed chief commissioner of Awadh; Brigadier General Sir Henry Havelock, who repeatedly attempted to reach the besieged Residency and finally succeeded; Sir James Outram and Sir Colin Campbell, who recaptured the city, and the controversial Brigadier William Hodson. Many of the sites so fiercely defended, so desperately attacked, so poignant in their ruined state, still exist today. This book tells the story of those places and the people who fought and died there.

Much was destroyed by the British after their recapture of the city in March 1858. The intricate passageways and little courts that wound through the riverbank palaces were all swept away. New roads were thrust through the garden palaces, dividing them in two. But the Residency compound, here called the garrison, was scrupulously preserved as a monument to the endurance of those besieged within it during the summer and autumn of 1857.

The city at peace. Lucknow in 1856. Ahmad Ali Khan.

Lucknow forms only a chapter in the history of the Uprising but it is an important chapter and by concentrating solely on the city, a more detailed picture of what happened there can be drawn.

Rosie Llewellyn-Jones
London, February 2022

1

Setting the Stage

THERE WERE A NUMBER OF causes of the Uprising, also known as the Indian Mutiny, the Sepoy Rebellion or sometimes the First War of Independence, although the latter name is disputed. What began as an army mutiny, when Indian soldiers turned on their British officers, quickly became a revolt against British rule, which spread across northern India. It started in May 1857 and was concluded by November 1858 with a general amnesty when the British government took over from the English East India Company. This was the start of the 'British Raj' or rule, which lasted until Independence. Lucknow was the capital of Awadh (also Oudh or Oude), a small kingdom that would fit comfortably into today's Uttar Pradesh. There was a specific reason for the Uprising here and this was the annexation of the kingdom of Awadh by the East India Company, followed by radical and unpopular reforms.

Battles

Four major military events took place near and in Lucknow, which will be examined in detail in this book. They were:

30 June 1857:	The Battle of Chinhat
25 September 1857:	The first (unsuccessful) relief of the Residency
14–22 November 1857:	The second (successful) relief of the Residency
4–19 March 1858:	The recapture of Lucknow

The siege of the Residency began on the night of 30 June and lasted for four and a half months until mid-November 1857. Although there was almost constant bombardment of the entire Residency area (around 33 acres) by Indian groups outside the perimeter and counter-attacks by those within, there were no pitched battles on the site.

Background to the conflict

Awadh had been ruled by the nawab wazirs, on behalf of the Mughal emperors, since 1720. The word nawab comes from the Persian 'na'ib' which means deputy. The first nawab, Burhan-ul-Mulk, had migrated from Naishapur in eastern Persia and became a trusted officer at the Mughal court in Delhi. When he was sent as governor to the province of Awadh to rule on the emperor's behalf, Burhan-ul-Mulk realized that the once-great Mughals were rapidly losing their grip on power in India. Awadh was one of three provinces that now became independent of the empire. Burhan-ul-Mulk's descendants were to rule Awadh for the next 136 years, until it was annexed by the East

India Company in February 1856. The seventh nawab, Ghazi-ud-din Haider, had been offered the title of 'king' by the Company in order to bind him more closely to the British. There was no real change in his status, except that the nawabs now became kings and Awadh was therefore referred to as 'the kingdom'. A British Resident, appointed by the Company to report back on the ruler and the court, lived in the Residency with his own large entourage and to many observers it seemed as if there were two centres of power in Lucknow—the king and the Resident.

The British Residency before the siege. Charles Ball, *History of the Indian Mutiny*, 1858.

Awadh had long been attractive to the East India Company, which had been making territorial gains in India since the mid-eighteenth century. It was a rich, fertile province lying in the Gangetic plain, which generated large sums of money for the nawabs from land revenue with smaller amounts coming from taxes on transport, trade and markets. After the capture of Delhi by the Company in 1803, Awadh acted as a geographical buffer between the old Mughal capital and the British capital at Calcutta. It was an annoying obstruction (in Company eyes) to its expansion into the Upper Provinces from its base in Bengal. Cawnpore (now Kanpur) and Allahabad, which had formerly been part of Awadh, had already been taken over by the Company but the bigger prize was Lucknow and the remaining territory of Awadh. The governor general, Lord Dalhousie, had pursued an aggressive forward policy during his time in office, deposing rulers and attaching kingdoms including the Punjab, to the Company's expanding portfolio. Dalhousie was due to leave India in March 1856 and he admitted privately that he would like to add Awadh to his tally before he went: 'I should not mind doing it as a parting coup,' he said.

The kingdom is taken over

In December 1855, Sir James Outram, the new British Resident, was instructed by Dalhousie to offer the king, Wajid Ali Shah, the unpalatable choice of voluntarily stepping down and handing his kingdom over to the Company or having it forcibly annexed. The king refused to step down and so Awadh passed into the Company's possession on 7 February 1856. There was none of the anticipated opposition at the time. The king had ordered his bodyguard to disarm and there was a mute, shocked silence as the Company took over the administration and began dismantling the trappings of royalty. Thirty thousand officers and men from the king's army were discharged and pensioned off, but allowed to keep their weapons, which they had brought with them on signing up. Many of these soldiers were to form part of the fighting force against the Company the following year. They were to become 'rebels' through no fault of their own.

A romanticized view of the British entry into Lucknow through the
Rumi Gate. Charles Ball, *History of the Indian Mutiny*, 1858.

Another unhappy group of people, and ready for a fight, were
the taluqdars, the landholders of Awadh. Company officials, newly
drafted in as administrators, had hastily passed the Summary Land
Settlement Act of 1856, which was an attempt to regulate the
collection of land revenue from the countryside. As a result, a number
of hereditary taluqdars had much of their land taken away and in
a few cases were actually imprisoned for debt because they could
not meet the Company's demands. Wealthy taluqdars could hold
considerable numbers of villages, as many as two hundred in some
cases. Revenue collecting runs right through the history of Awadh.
Money due to the treasury often had to be extracted by force when
landholders either refused to pay up, or were unable to do so. Soldiers
from the king's army were used to surround the mud-brick forts
which dotted the countryside, isolated by the surrounding jungle or

by deep trenches. Iron safes were cemented into the floors of the forts,
where specie was kept. The forts were guarded by part-time soldiers,
one or two hundred around the smaller structures but as many as
2,000 at larger establishments, with cavalry too. They could draw
on the fort's armoury for weapons, which included small cannon.
These private armies were paid directly by the taluqdar and so they
not only relied on him for a living, but had a certain loyalty to their
master as well. When some of the largest landowning taluqdars like
Raja Nawab Ali Khan of Mahmudabad, Loni Singh of Mitauli and
Raja Beni Madhao Singh of Amethi joined the Uprising in June 1857
and provided support to the still amorphous opposition gathering
around Lucknow, their private armies came with them too.

Mahmudabad Qila, a taluqdar stronghold about thirty miles from
Lucknow, 1976. Author's collection.

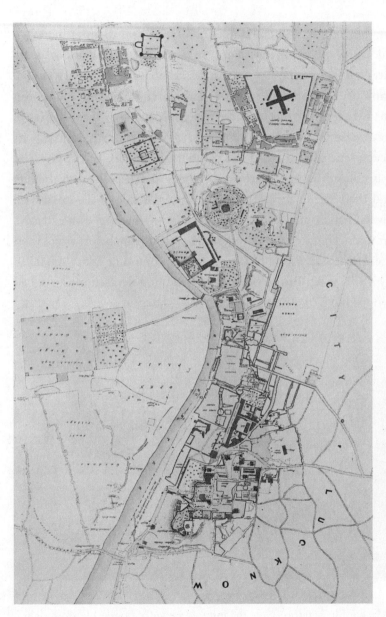

'Plan of the entrenched position of the British Garrison at Lucknow 1857'. Captain F.H.M. Sitwell. Scale 400 feet to 1 inch. Overall size: 26 inches x 40 inches.

The city of Lucknow

At the time of the Uprising, there were two distinct 'parts' to Lucknow, the old medieval area marked on British maps as 'dense city' and the new, post-1775 nawabi area that ran along the southern bank of the Gomti river. Three large palace complexes had been erected there, two of which, the Chattar Manzil and the Qaisarbagh, featured prominently in the Uprising. The Haider canal with its deeply cut sides marked the southern boundary of the city and was crossed by the Charbagh bridge, a pinch-point into the city and the scene of fierce fighting. On the far side of the canal were several handsome 'country houses' standing in their own extensive grounds. The city was not walled. The population before annexation is estimated by a local historian to be around nine lakh (900,000). By 1871, when British officials carried out a detailed census it had dropped to 370,000.

Macchi Bhawan fort. Note the inserted image of doors at bottom right.
1858. Felice Beato.

With one exception, all the fighting during the Uprising took
place in the new city—along Hazratganj, the broad highway lined
with palaces and imambaras (religious halls); around the British
Residency at the end of Hazratganj and at the country houses across
the canal. The medieval fort called Macchi Bhawan straddled both
old and new cities. It stood on a small prominence overlooking the
river Gomti and the Stone Bridge, one of two fixed crossing points
to the north bank. The Iron Bridge was the second. Although the
river was used extensively in the past when buildings along it had
their own river gates, there was also a network of roads radiating
out from the city. These were maintained in reasonable condition,
often at the insistence of the Company, which provided its own
engineers, but charged the nawabs for the work. The two vital links
for the Company were the road to Cawnpore, with its large British
cantonment along the bank of the Ganges, and the new road to the
smaller, local cantonment at Mariaon, four miles north of Lucknow.

Old tombs in the Mariaon cantonment cemetery today.
Anil Mehrotra.

It had not been the Company's choice to establish its cantonment so far away from the city, but this was all that was offered in 1807 when the nawab of the time, Saadat Ali Khan, refused to allocate a site nearer his capital. When the emergency came and the Mariaon cantonment was set alight on 30 May 1857, help only arrived the following day, and when disturbances broke out in Lucknow itself, these had to be dealt with by the city police, not the military.

The countryside around Lucknow is generally flat and the nearest hills of any size are two hundred miles east towards Chunar, with its quarries of fine-grained hard sandstone. This seems of little significance at first, but it meant the cost of bringing stone from Chunar was high, so the majority of Lucknow's buildings were constructed from locally made brick, called lakhori, which was to affect the relief of the city in 1857 and its recapture the following year. Buildings constructed of thousands of small baked bricks, with exterior walls over two feet deep, are not easily penetrated. They cannot be set on fire and they will not easily shatter under cannon fire.

Conclusion

The deposed king, with a sizeable retinue of wives, relatives, servants and personal bodyguards, left Lucknow on 13 March 1856. His intention was to travel to England to meet Queen Victoria and plead for the annexation to be reversed. He took no overt part in the Uprising and in fact offered military support to the Company, which was not accepted.[1] The Uprising in Awadh had specific causes. It was not an attempt to expel the East India Company from India. It was a much more domestic affair—Awadh wanted its old regime back and the Company's outrageous revenue demands cancelled. Post-Uprising rationalization may claim this as India's First War of

Independence from colonial rule but in truth there was no sense at the time of India as a whole. The word 'Hindustan' applied only to northern India and sometimes only to the area around Delhi itself. To the south lay the Deccan, untouched during the Uprising, Bengal to the east where no attempt was made to storm the British capital and the conquered Punjab to the north-west.

2

The Warring Sides

FIGHTING IN LUCKNOW DURING THE Uprising did not follow the conventional pattern of warfare. It was not like the Battle of Plassey, exactly a hundred years earlier, where two opposing bodies of soldiers met each other on open ground. Apart from the brief Battle of Chinhat that marked the start of hostilities, fighting took place in urban spaces—along residential streets, in religious buildings, in palace gardens, in a school, on a bridge, in houses and sometimes even from room to room. In spite of fierce resistance put up by Indian soldiers (sepoys) the eventual outcome was not in doubt at the end of March 1858. Ironically, the East India Company won the conflict but lost the peace because it was abolished at the end of that year and its former territories came under direct rule by the British government.

The Indian force

Descriptions of men fighting against the British and Company troops are often vague—they are referred to as 'the rebels', 'the rebel sepoys', 'the mutineers' or simply 'the enemy'. After some of the Company's own sepoy regiments mutinied, identification could be refined: 'disloyal men of the 48th Bengal Native Infantry', for example. In spite of much research in recent years by Indian scholars, the history of the Uprising is still told largely by the victors—the British—and complemented by the accounts of British civilians. A list (compiled by British intelligence at the end of 1857) gives the most detailed breakdown of the men who opposed the first and second reliefs of the British Residency garrison. They deserve to be remembered no less than the Britons who fell during the conflict. And because nothing is ever simple in India, there are also sepoys killed by their fellow countrymen because they were fighting *for* the Company, not against it, and a couple of Europeans fighting *with* the rebels, and against the Company.

Wajid Ali Shah inspecting his troops c. 1848.
Hussainabad Picture Gallery, Lucknow.

On his accession in 1847 the new king, Wajid Ali Shah, enthusiastically took command of the Awadh army, at first holding regular inspections and establishing new regiments. But he was discouraged by successive British Residents and soon abandoned this early interest. His army of 60,350 officers and men was disbanded after annexation, and less than half its soldiers re-absorbed into the new Oudh Irregular Force and the Oudh Military Police Force set up by the Company. Many of the men in these two units were to desert and join the rebels. It is also clear that during the first six months of 1857 some of the king's disbanded regiments were secretly regrouping. Some even kept their old names, like the Akhtari (Star-like) Pultan, taken over by Captain Fida Hussain and Captain Bhowani Singh, which expanded to a regiment of over 1,550 troops. The Tirchha (Perverse) Regiment, commanded by Diyanat-ud-daula, reformed after the eunuch left Lucknow to accompany his king to Calcutta (now Kolkata). Two regiments, both captained by country-born Britons who officially retired on annexation, retained their former officers' names—Barlow's Regiment after Captain Charles Grant Barlow, now led by Captain Umrao Singh, and Bunbury's Regiment, after Captain Abraham Charles Bunbury, now led by Captain Makhdoom Baksh. Before annexation, other Europeans had commanded platoons or companies for the king: William Hearsey, Alexander Orr and Captain Magness had each led a jamiat (company) of soldiers, drilling them in English and teaching their bandsmen to play English tunes. We have already noted the considerable numbers of armed men that the taluqdars brought with them to Lucknow. These three elements—mutinous soldiers from Company regiments, reformed regiments from the king's disbanded army and the taluqdars' men—united to make up the Indian force.

Renegades

There were a few people during the Uprising who didn't fall neatly into the expected categories. These were Europeans and Anglo-Indians who fought *for* the rebels and against the British. Captain Felix Rotton was the son of an English father and an Indian mother and was well into his sixties when the mutiny broke out. He was said to have become a Muslim and to have been employed by the nawabs as an artillery commander. Felix had fathered a large number of children by various Indian women and married his daughters to Muslim men while his sons served as officers in the nawab's army. Seven of his sons joined the Lucknow rebels and fought against the British. Three of them, James, John and Joseph, were killed during the hostilities. Felix himself refused to seek refuge in the Residency and remained living in the city during the siege. He joined Begam Hazrat Mahal during her flight to Nepal but surrendered to the British in July 1858. His case was thoroughly investigated by the chief commissioner who found no evidence that he had actually taken part in any fighting, unlike his sons, so he was released.

Another case, with an unhappier ending, was that of Captain Savary, a retired invalid officer of the Bengal Native Infantry who, like Felix Rotton, was a long-time resident in Lucknow. Savary had married the daughter of a high-ranking Indian military officer from Malihabad, and had converted to Islam. He 'mixed familiarly with native society' and was sometimes called upon by the British Resident at court for his local knowledge.

Savary had become thoroughly Indianized (gone native, as the British would say) and he offended the Residents by turning up in native dress at the Residency. He was last consulted by Henry Lawrence at the end of May 1857 when he did manage to wear 'European costume' but he seemed ill and out of sorts, according to Martin Gubbins, who was present at the meeting.

Savary was subsequently arrested by rebel soldiers and even though he showed them a declaration that he was a Muslim (probably by reciting the kalimah) he was hauled off to a prominent Shi'a cleric to verify his statement. Something went wrong along the way and Savary was killed by his captors who then looted his city house.

'The Dawn of Victory', Colin Campbell and officers on 14 November 1857. Oil painting by Thomas Barker, c. 1862. National Army Museum, London.

Commanders and Objectives

By the end of June 1857 leaders were emerging from the disparate groups, although no commander-in-chief was appointed and there was as yet no figurehead to unite them. A number of pre-emptive arrests had been made in Lucknow by the British Resident, which included relatives of the Mughal emperor, Bahadur Shah Zafar, the nominal head of the Uprising. The king had left many of his own relatives behind in Lucknow when he travelled to Calcutta, and his elder brother, two nephews and a niece were confined in the Residency during the siege. Also arrested in June was Nawab Rukn-ud-daula, a potential leader related to the king's family, who had already started a military training camp in the old city for rebel recruits. Out in the countryside, the taluqdars' armies were beginning to assemble at Nawabganj, some eighteen miles east of Lucknow on the Faizabad Road.

Two men from very different backgrounds were prominent at the start of the Uprising: Raja Nawab Ali Khan of Mahmudabad, a respected taluqdar who was able to bring over 2,000 fighting men with him, and the maulvi (priest) Ahmadullah Shah, also known as Danka Shah, whose background was mysterious, and who may have visited England and had some military training. On hearing of the outbreak on 10 May 1857, soldiers around Lucknow, who were not yet in revolt but ripe for mutiny, planned to march to Delhi to join comrades from Meerut, who had arrived there after an all-night march. According to local historians, Raja Mahmudabad and Khan Ali Khan, a former official of the Company, persuaded the soldiers against the march and urged them instead to lay siege to the Britons in Lucknow. The psychological impact on men who had seized the whole of Awadh but were now confined to a mere thirty-three acres of its capital was promoted and the raja's reasoning prevailed. It was planned to frighten the British into surrendering, which would have had an important symbolic effect throughout northern India. This does seem borne out by the steady concentration of rebel forces towards Lucknow, after isolated Britons in out-stations had either been killed or had fled. The question of whether those within the garrison would have been killed, like their Cawnpore counterparts, had the site been overrun, has never been asked, nor answered.

Birjis Qadr, the boy king crowned in 1857. Artist unknown.

Meanwhile a royal figurehead was sought, one closely related
to the absent king. Raja Jai Lal Singh (also Jia Lal), an Awadh
taluqdar with a town house in Lucknow, was deputed to find a
suitable candidate. The eldest son of the king was considered, but
he was disabled and too unfit. Another son, the twelve-year-old
Birjis Qadr, was chosen and crowned with a simple turban. But it
was his mother, Begam Hazrat Mahal, who became the chief figure
of the resistance and is as celebrated today as is the Rani of Jhansi.
Birjis Qadr's appointment was not as a military leader—this role was
quickly taken on by his mother and her advisors. He was needed
as nominal head of the city's administration which had collapsed
after the Company's defeat at Chinhat. The soldiers who poured
into Lucknow after the British lost control went on an orgy of
looting and destruction, ransacking shops and the houses of wealthy
townsmen, and digging up their gardens in the search for treasure.
Gradually order was restored and a military junta set up called
Sazman-Jawanan-e-Awadh (Organization of Awadh Soldiers). The
eclectic maulvi who had installed himself in the old observatory,
the Tarawali Kothi, was not initially invited to join the junta and
when he did there was friction between him and the begam. But by
'his forceful personality, holy character and military judgement [he]
commanded increasing support from all sections of the army'. So
Raja Jai Lal Singh was designated army commandant, Begam Hazrat
Mahal represented (on behalf of her son) the royal family of Awadh,
and the maulvi began to call himself the viceregent of God—a trinity
of military, royal and religious opposition that planned to humiliate
the British into surrender.

Begam Hazrat Mahal
c. 1820–1879

Many myths attach to the begam, who was a divorced wife of the last king, Wajid Ali Shah. She was the daughter of an African slave called Amber and his partner Maher Afza. Amber was owned by Mir Ghulam Hossein Ali Khan who had connections with Faizabad, the old capital of Awadh. The handsome young woman entered the king's music academy, the Pari Khana, around 1840, when the king made a grant of land to her father, thus freeing him from slavery.[2] She was named Mahak Pari or Fragrant Fairy and when she became pregnant by the king in 1845, he gave her the title of Nawab Iftikhar un-nissa, 'Proud among women'. When her son was born later that year, he was given the title of Mirza Birjis Qadr. His mother was elevated to the rank of *mahal,* a woman who has given birth to a king's son. Hazrat was a popular name in Lucknow (the main street is called Hazratganj), with religious and royal connotations. Begam is the respectful term for a married woman, so Begam Hazrat Mahal emerges, a former dancing girl, mother of the king's fourth son, and his thirteenth wife. (Wajid Ali Shah was to marry 370 women during the course of his life.)

In 1850, the king's mother insisted that Wajid Ali Shah divorce Begam Hazrat Mahal and eight more of his wives on spurious grounds. Her real objection was that the begam and the others were of lowly birth and not fitting companions for a king. When Wajid Ali Shah left Lucknow in March 1856, Begam Hazrat Mahal was left behind with her young son. She was initially reluctant to let him become the nominal head of

Wajid Ali Shah and Begam Hazrat Mahal, from the *Ishqnama*, c. 1845. Windsor Castle, Royal Collection Trust, copyright Her Majesty Queen Elizabeth II, 2020.

government but after his coronation, the begam too became an important figurehead in the fight against the British.

After the recapture of Lucknow, mother and son fled to Nepal, where Jang Bahadur, their former opponent, reluctantly gave them shelter, his reluctance eased by the royal jewels the begam had managed to bring with her. She is buried in Kathmandu. Birjis Qadr was allowed to return to India in 1887 where he was later allegedly poisoned by jealous family members.

The British force

Because Awadh had been peacefully annexed by the Company in February 1856 the military aspect of the occupation was played down. Decent administration and good leadership were considered the key to a successful takeover. Awadh was split into four divisions, each with a commissioner, and each division was subdivided into three districts with a deputy commissioner—a total of sixteen major British officials with their own staff and often with their families as well to emphasize the 'normal' nature of the new regime. Major John Sherbrooke Banks, appointed Commissioner Lucknow Division, deliberately chose to set up his new office outside the Residency, to signal a break with the past. He moved into a large bungalow built over an eighteenth-century powder mill, which became known as Banks's Bungalow. To provide quiet reassurance HM 32nd Regiment of Foot, approximately 500 officers and men, were drafted in, the only British regiment in Awadh. An old palace, the Khurshid Manzil, was requisitioned to become the Officers' Mess. The men of this regiment were housed in the Chaupar elephant stables, north of Hazratganj. There were also three well-established Company regiments of Indian sepoys led by British officers, the 13th, the 48th and the 71st Bengal Native Infantry, some units of which were quartered in the distant Mariaon cantonment, and others even further north at Mudkipur. In addition, there were regiments of Military Police, and regiments of the Oudh Irregular Infantry, which had recruited men from the king's army when it was disbanded. Because the annexation took place in February at the start of the hot season there had been no time to erect new buildings for the troops, so existing properties had to be requisitioned, including palaces and a large tomb called Shah Najaf, the burial place of the seventh nawab. Overlooking the tomb and standing proud on a small artificial hill was the Qadam-i-Rasool, a building that housed a reputed footprint of the Prophet.

Unwisely, this was used by the British as a powder magazine, which naturally alienated the townspeople. It was admitted by the financial commissioner, Martin Gubbins, that there was a 'very faulty and irregular distribution of troops and military stores' but at the same time he reported that 'the condition of the Province of Oudh was perfectly tranquil. No breeze ruffled the serenity of the still water.' Company officials planned to sort out army accommodation during the next cold-weather season, little knowing that by then they would be fighting for their lives.

'The Kudmsee Russol' [Qadam-i-Rasool], 1858. Felice Beato.
Getty Images.

At the end of April 1857, in the last days of peace, there were 4,000 Indian troops stationed in and around the city. Two months later only about 650 men remained loyal to the Company. The rest had deserted, or had been dismissed to their homes in a bid to avert trouble. What the British hadn't reckoned on was that the majority of people in Awadh preferred to be governed, however poorly, by their own king, rather than being, as the British perceived, better governed by foreigners. It was a mistake born of arrogance that led to Lucknow becoming a battlefield.

Sir Henry Lawrence arrived in Lucknow at the end of March 1857 as the newly appointed chief commissioner of Awadh. He was a seasoned soldier in the Company's army and had served in the Anglo-Afghan War and the capture of the Punjab. He had been British Resident in Kathmandu and the Political Agent in Rajputana, both civil administrative posts. Now as chief commissioner he had both military and civil authority and the title Brigadier General. Although in poor health, he commanded the British and Company forces in Awadh until he was killed at the beginning of July 1857. His second in command was Colonel John Inglis of HM 32nd Regiment. Lawrence's objective before the Battle of Chinhat was a pre-emptive strike on rebel soldiers attempting to enter Lucknow from their headquarters at Nawabganj. His failure marked the start of the siege of the Residency.

Sir Henry Lawrence, c. 1856. Walker & Boutall, National Army Museum, London.

Brigadier General Sir Henry Havelock, commanding the Oudh Field Force, led the first relief of the Residency in September 1857. Arriving in India in 1823, Havelock fought in major battles as the Company expanded into Burma and the Punjab. He also commanded troops in the First Afghan War (1839–42) and the Anglo-Persian War of 1857. From here he was recalled to India, marching west from the headquarters at Allahabad to Cawnpore, arriving a day after the massacre of British women and children. He then made three attempts to reach Lucknow and having finally got to the Residency on the fourth attempt, did not have sufficient manpower to bring out those besieged, so the main objective of his mission failed.

Major General Sir James Outram and **Field Marshall Colin Campbell** led the second relief into the city in mid-November 1857 where they joined forces with Havelock. The besieged soldiers and civilians were successfully evacuated to safety via Cawnpore and Allahabad. A small force remained at Alambagh, south of Lucknow, with Outram—too weak to recapture the city but strong enough to repel rebel attacks. By the beginning of March 1858 British Company and Gurkha forces were assembled and Lucknow was successfully recaptured by 19 March, achieving the objective set them by governor general, Lord Canning, who had insisted that this was the key to subduing the mutiny.

Orders of Battle

Battle of Chinhat, 30 June 1857

Indian forces

Commanders (Infantry): Khan Ali Khan, Maulvi Ahmadullah Shah and Raja Jai Lal Singh
Commander (Cavalry): General Burkat Ahmed (*risaldar* of the 15th Bengal Irregular Cavalry)

Trained infantry (about 5,500 men)

22nd Bengal Native Infantry (Faizabad)
2nd, 3rd, 5th, 6th, 8th and 9th Oude Irregular Infantry, from Secrora, Gonda, Dariabad, Faizabad, Sultanpur and Sitapur
1st and 2nd Regiments Military Police, from Sultanpur and Sitapur

Trained cavalry (about 800 men)

Officers: Risaldar Saugan Singh, Risaldar Sarjan Singh, Risaldar Faqir Mohamed Goya, Ausan Singh, Bahadur Ali, Risaldar Ismail Khan, Risaldar Pir Zahur Ali , Ghamandi Singh (of Captain Alexander Orr's regiment), Rajmund Tiwari (Bole Regiment)

15th Bengal Irregular Cavalry

Bulk of 1st, 2nd and 3rd Oude Irregular Cavalry (local regiments—Daly's, Gall's and Hardinge's)

Some Military Police under Captain Raghunath Singh and Captain Umrao Singh

Taluqdar forces

Raja Nawab Ali Khan, Mahmudabad
Raja Beni Madho Singh, Amethi

Artillery

12 pieces from 5th Company/7th Battalion with No. 13 Field Battery, Bengal Artillery. Horse-drawn Light Field Battery, 9-pounder
No. 1 Light Field Battery, Oudh Irregular Artillery. Horse-drawn Light Field Battery, 9-pounder
4 x light guns. Type unknown. Possibly 6-pounders

Total, excluding artillery officers and crews, and taluqdars' private armies: 6,300.

British and Company forces

Commander: Brigadier-General Sir Henry Lawrence, chief commissioner of Awadh
Second in command: Colonel John Inglis, HM 32nd Regiment
Officer commanding the artillery: Captain Alfred Simons

Infantry (530 men)

HM 32nd Regiment: Lieutenant Colonel William Case
13th Bengal Native Infantry: Major C.F. Bruere
48th Bengal Native Infantry: Lieutenant-Colonel H. Palmer
71st Bengal Native Infantry (Sikhs): Lieutenant J.M. Birch/ Lieutenant-Colonel Halford

Cavalry (156 men)

Volunteer Horse (European): Captain C.W. Radcliffe
Detachments of 1st, 2nd and 3rd Oude Irregular Cavalry: Lieutenant
G. Hardinge

Artillery

4 x guns Horse Light Field Battery: Lieutenant F.J. Cunliffe
4 x guns No. 2 Oudh Light Field Battery: Lieutenant D. MacFarlan
2 x guns No. 3 Oudh Field Battery: Lieutenant Ashe and Lieutenant
J.H. Bryce
1 x 8-inch howitzer: Lieutenant J. Bonham

Total, excluding artillery officers and crews: 686.

Indian forces during the first and second reliefs, September and November 1857

Description	Strength
Infantry regiments	
Captains Suba Singh and Akipal Singh	700
No. 8 Right Wing: Captain Gajadhar Singh	799
Nadir Shahi Regiment: Seetul Singh	400
Barlow's Regiment: Captain Umrao Singh	700
Akhtari Regiment: Captain Fida Hussain	600
Right Wing of the Akhtari Regiment: Captain Bhowani Singh	950
Volunteers (37th N.I.): Captain Gauri Shanker	750
Bole Regiment (22nd N.I.): Captain Rakam Tiwari	700
8th Oude Locals: Captain Makhdoom Baksh	700
Robert's Regiment	1,150

Regiment No. 9: Captain Gajen Singh	600
General Agha Hussain	400
General Jafir Ali	350
General Sheik Ali Baqar	400
General Bahadur Ali	250
General Mir Naqi Ali Khan	762
General Mirza Shaharyar	882
Remnants of other regiments from the king's army	2,556

Cavalry regiments

Regiment No. 12: Captain Hari Singh	700
Regiment No. 15	800
Regiment. No. 11	600
Talwar Khan Risaladar's Regiment	500
Tirchha Regiment	700
Maiman-i-Shahi Regiment	700
Mesurrah Regiment	900
Ali Baksh Khan's Regiment	800
Mahomed Akbar's Regiment	900
New Regiment	120

Taluqdars' troops

Raja Hardat Singh Bahadur, Bahraich	200
Raghunath Singh, Raipur	200
Ikauna Men	240
Ghangapur Men	150
Hardar Singh, Churda	300

Tepurdha Men	100
Balrajkumar Men	200
Shahpur Men	100
Kishandatt Pandey's Men	1,200
Sadun Salgunge	1,000
Bhinga Men	800
Tulsipur Men	500
Nanpara Men	400
Raghunath Singh, Baiswara	1,000
Raja of Tiloi Shanker Singh	80
Sheo Shankar Singh, Jorapur	500
Lal Bahadur, Kalakunkur	1,000
Rampur Katowalah Men	400
Raja Beni Madho Singh, Amethi	3,500
Raja Man Singh	7,000
Raja Sahab Ram, Banthra	2,000
Raja Gurbux Singh, Ramnagar	2,500
Raja Nawab Ali Khan, Mahmudabad	2,200
Raja Bazljandur Singh, Palpur	1,500
Surajput Burhila	2,000
Baley Dube, Amaura	100
Umrao Singh, Mauhar	500
Umrao Singh, Ajuldhukwa	500
Jai Narain Singh, Dhaurauwa	300
Balpur Rao, Khairabad	800
Jai Pradash, Isanagar	500
Total:	**53,350**

British and Company forces: First relief of Lucknow, 25 September 1857

The Oudh Field Force (Allahabad Moveable Column) Commander: Brigadier-General Sir Henry Havelock
Chief Commissioner Oudh: Major-General Sir James Outram
Military Secretary: Colonel Robert Napier, Bengal Engineers
Deputy Assistant Quartermaster General: Colonel Fraser Tytler
Deputy Assistant Adjutant General: Lieutenant Henry (Harry) Havelock
Chief Engineer: Captain William Crommelin

Infantry

1st Infantry Brigade: Brigadier James Neill
HM 5th Regiment (Northumberland Fusiliers): Major James Simmons. Nos. 1, 2, 3, 6, 8, 9 and 10 Cos.
HM 84th (York and Lancaster) Regiment and HM 64th (2 Cos.): Captain Frederic Willis
1st Madras Fusiliers ('Neill's Bluecaps'): Major John Stephenson
2nd Infantry Brigade: Brigadier Walter Hamilton, 78th Highlanders
HM 78th Highlanders (Ross-shire Buffs): Lieutenant-Colonel Henry Stisted
HM 90th (Perthshire Volunteers) (Light Infantry): Colonel Robert Campbell
Ferozepore Regiment (Brasyer's Sikhs): Captain Jeremiah Brasyer
6th Bengal Native Infantry (BNI) (mostly Sikhs): Captain William Johnson

Cavalry

5th Madras Light Cavalry: Captain Lousada Barrow

Allahabad Volunteer Cavalry
12th Bengal Irregular Cavalry

Artillery

3rd Artillery Brigade: Brigadier George Cooper. 18 guns
Maude's Battery, No. 3 Company/8th Battalion, Royal Artillery:
Captain Francis Maude. Bullock-drawn field battery. 5 x 9-pounders,
1 x 24-pounder
Olpherts' Battery, No. 2 Company/3rd Battalion with No. 12 Light
Field Battery, Bengal Artillery: Captain William Olpherts. Horse-
drawn 5 x 9-pounders, 1 x 24-pounder
Eyre's Battery, No. 3 Heavy Field Battery, Bengal Artillery: Major
Vincent Eyre. Bullock-drawn 4 x 24-pounders, 2 x 8-inch howitzers.

Total: European infantry 2,388, Sikh infantry 341, European
volunteer cavalry 109, Sikh irregular horse 59, gunners 282.

British and Company forces: Second relief of Lucknow, 14–22 November 1857

Commander-in-Chief India: General Sir Colin Campbell
Chief of Staff: Major General William Mansfield
Divisional Commander: Major-General Hope Grant
OC Royal Artillery: Captain Frederick Travers
OC Bengal Artillery: Major Frank Turner

Infantry

3rd Infantry Brigade: Brigadier Edward Greathed, HM 8th
Regiment
HM 8th Regiment: Major John Hinde

Hamilton's 1st Battalion of Detachments: Lieutenant Colonel Henry Hamilton
2nd (Green's) Punjab Infantry: Captain George Green
4th Infantry Brigade: Brigadier the Hon. Adrian Hope, HM 93rd Highlanders
HM 93rd Highlanders: Lieutenant Colonel Alexander Leith Hay
HM 53rd Regiment: Lieutenant Colonel Charles Gordon
4th (Wilde's) Punjab Infantry: A/Captain William Paul, 7th BNI
2nd Battalion of Detachments: Major Roger Barnston
5th Infantry Brigade: Brigadier David Russell, 84th Regiment
HM 23rd Regiment: Lieutenant-Colonel Samuel Wells
HM 82nd Regiment: Lieutenant-Colonel Edward Hale

Cavalry

Cavalry Brigade: Brigadier Archibald Little
HM 9th Lancers: Major Henry Ouvry
2nd Battalion Military Train: Major James Robertson
1st Punjab Cavalry: Lieutenant John Watson
2nd Punjab Cavalry: Lieutenant Dighton Probyn
5th Punjab Cavalry: Lieutenant George Younghusband, 13th BNI

Naval Brigade (HMS *Shannon*): Captain William Peel. Bullock-drawn guns: 6 x 24-pounders, 2 x 8-inch howitzers, 2 x rocket carts

Artillery

Artillery Brigade: Brigadier William Crawford
Hardy's Battery: Captain Whaley Hardy. Heavy Field Battery: 2 x 18-pounders, 1 x 8-inch howitzer
Longden's Battery: Captain Charles Longden. 6 x 8-inch mortars, 10 x 5.5-inch mortars

Middleton's Battery: Captain William Middleton. Horse-drawn Field
Battery. 4 x 9-pounders, 2 x 24-pounder howitzers
Remmington's Troop: Captain Frederick Remmington. 4 x
6-pounders, 1 x 12-pounder howitzer
Blunt's Troop: Captain Charles Blunt. 4 x 9-pounders, 1 x
24-pounder howitzer
1 x division E Troop, Madras Horse Artillery: Lieutenant C. Bridge.
2 x 6-pounders
Captain George Bourchier. Horse-drawn Light Field Battery. 4 x
9-pounders, 2 x 24-pounder howitzers

Engineers

Madras Engineers: Lieutenant Scott
Royal Engineers: Lieutenant Wilbraham Lennox
1 Co. Madras Sappers and Miners
Detachment Bengal Sappers and Miners
2 Cos. Punjab Sappers and Miners

Total: Cavalry 860, naval brigade 250, infantry 4,480, engineers
380; excludes artillery.

Indian forces: Recapture of Lucknow 4–19 March 1858

Commander: Begam Hazrat Mahal
Commander: Maulvi Ahmadullah Shah

1st Division	Delhi Force under Muzaffar Jahan. 2,424 men, 360 horses, no guns
2nd Division	Magribi under Raja Jai Lal Singh. 6,403 men, 360 horses, 5 guns
3rd Division	Najeebs under Hisam ud-daula. 12,544 men, 4,655 horses, 60 guns

4th Division   Maulvi Ahmadullah Shah. 8,310 men, 150 horses, 6 guns

Taluqdar Force   Nawab Ali Khan, Mahmudabad. 2,200 men, 120 horses, 2 guns

Total: Men 36,237, horses 5,828, artillery 127

British, Company and Gurkha forces: Recapture of Lucknow 4–19 March 1858

Commander-in-Chief: General Sir Colin Campbell
Chief of Staff: Major-General William Mansfield
Military Secretary: Colonel C.A.F. Berkeley, HM 32nd Regiment

Divisional Commanders
1st Division: Sir James Outram
2nd Division: Major-General Sir Edward Lugard
3rd Division: Brigadier-General Robert Walpole
4th Division: Brigadier-General Sir Thomas Franks
Cavalry Division: Major-General Sir J. Hope Grant
Artillery Division: Major-General Sir Archdale Wilson

Infantry

1st Division
    1st Infantry Brigade: Brigadier D. Russell
        HM 84th Regiment of Foot
        HM 5th Fusiliers 1st Battalion
        1st Madras Fusiliers, Regiment

    2nd Infantry Brigade
        HM 90th Light Infantry: Lieutenant Harry Havelock
        HM 78th Highlanders: Captain Macpherson

Regiment of Ferozepore including Brasyer's Sikhs

2nd Division
  3rd Infantry Brigade: Brigadier P.M.M. Guy
    HM 34th Regiment: Acting Brigadier Lieutenant-Colonel
    R.D. Kelly
    HM 38th Regiment
    HM 53rd Regiment

  4th Infantry Brigade: Brigadier the Hon. Adrian Hope
    HM 42nd Royal Highlanders
    HM 53rd Regiment: Lieutenant-Colonel English
    HM 30th Regiment
    HM 90th Regiment
    HM 93rd Highlanders
    4th Punjab Rifles (64th NI)

3rd Division
  5th Infantry Brigade: Brigadier Douglas
    HM 23rd Royal Welsh Fusiliers
    HM 79th Highlanders
    1st European Bengal Fusiliers: Lieutenant Butler

  6th Infantry Brigade: Brigadier Horsford
    HM 23rd Foot
    HM 79th Highlanders: Lieutenant Colonel Taylor
    HM 22nd Royal Welsh Fusiliers
    and one company under Captain Salisbury
    2nd Battalion Rifle Brigade: Lieutenant-Colonel Percy Hill
    3rd Battalion Rifle Brigade: Lieutenant-Colonel MacDonell
    2nd Punjab Infantry: Lieutenant-Colonel Pratt

4th Division
7th Infantry Brigade: Brigadier Evelegh
    HM 10th Regiment of Foot
    HM 20th Regiment: Captain Bennett
    HM 90th Regiment
    HM 97th Regiment
    Gurkha Force [separate from Jang Bahadur's Gurkhas]

Cavalry

1st Cavalry Brigade
    Pathan Horse
    HM 9th Lancers
    2nd Punjab Cavalry
    5th Punjab Irregular Cavalry (detachment): Major Sandford
    1st Sikh Irregular Cavalry (Wale's Horse)
    2nd Battalion Military Train
    12th Irregular Cavalry (detachment) and Oudh Irregular
    Cavalry

2nd Cavalry Brigade
    HM 7th Hussars
    HM 7th Queen's Own Hussars
    HM 2nd Dragoon Guards: Lieutenant-Colonel Briscoe
    Volunteer Cavalry
    Hodson's Horse: Brigadier William Hodson
    Detachments of Benares Horse, Lahore Light Horse, Pathan
    Horse, 3rd Sikh Irregular Cavalry, 1st Punjab Cavalry

Artillery Division

Naval Brigade (HMS *Shannon*): Captain William Peel
Field Artillery: Captain Middleton

1st Brigade
   2nd Troop, Bengal Horse Artillery
   No. 20 Light Field Battery: Captain Gibbon
3rd Brigade Bengal Horse Artillery
   3rd Troop, Bengal Horse Artillery

Royal Artillery, 12th Battalion, 5th Co.
   F. Troop, Royal Horse Artillery
   Lieutenant-Colonel D'Aguilar's Troop Horse Artillery

Siege Artillery: Lieutenant-Colonel Riddell
   Royal Artillery, 11th Battalion, 6th Co.
   Bengal Artillery, 5th Battalion, 3rd Co.
   Royal Artillery, 8th Battalion, 3rd Co.
   Royal Artillery, 2nd Battalion, 8th Co.
   Royal Artillery, 14th Battalion, 3rd Co.
   Royal Artillery, 13th Battalion, 6th Co.
   1st Brigade Horse Artillery, 1st Troop

Engineer Brigade
   4th Co. Royal Engineers
   23rd Co. Royal Engineers
   Bengal Engineers (doing duty with Royal Engineers)
   Bengal Sappers and Miners
   Punjab Pioneers
   Punjab Sappers
   Delhi Pioneers

Jang Bahadur's Gurkhas—six battalions of infantry and artillery (8,000 men)

Total: 33,664 men with 164 pieces of artillery.

3

Chronology of Dates and Events

1856

7 February: East India Company annexes the kingdom of Awadh.
13 March: The king of Awadh, Wajid Ali Shah, leaves Lucknow for Calcutta.

1857

1 May: new recruits to the 7th Oudh Irregular Infantry at Mariaon refuse cartridges. Twenty mutinous soldiers hanged at Macchi Bhawan.

30 May: Mariaon cantonment set on fire and soldiers mutiny. Members of the royal family arrested. Electric telegraph cut.

3 June: Infantry units and Military Police mutiny at Sitapur, 50 miles north of Lucknow; 14 Europeans and many Indian Christians murdered

30 June: Battle of Chinhat. Sir Henry Lawrence with 600 soldiers defeated at Ismaelganj (Chinhat) by 5,000 Indian troops. Retreats to the Residency and the siege begins.

4 July: Sir Henry Lawrence dies from wounds in the Residency.

25 September: First relief of Lucknow. Brigadier-General Henry Havelock and Sir James Outram fight their way into the Residency with heavy loss of life and decide to wait there for reinforcements.

14–22 November: Second relief of Lucknow. Commander-in-Chief Sir Colin Campbell fights his way into Lucknow and captures the riverside palaces. Fierce fighting inside Sikanderbagh. Women, children and the wounded evacuated from the Residency garrison on 19 November.

'The 93rd Highlanders entering the Breach at the storming of the Secundrabagh'. Watercolour by Orlando Norie, 1858. National Army Museum, London.

23 November: Rebel soldiers enter the empty Residency garrison and loot it.

24 November: Brigadier-General Sir Henry Havelock dies of dysentery at Dilkusha Palace.

1858

4 March: Recapture of Lucknow begins under command of Sir Colin Campbell.

12 March: Jang Bahadur, the Nepalese leader, arrives with about 8,000 Gurkhas to support British troops.

14 March: British and Company troops capture Qaisarbagh Palace. Begam Hazrat Mahal flees to Musa Bagh. Looting of palace lasts for two days.

19 March: Lucknow secured by British, Company and Gurkha troops. Final showdown at Musa Bagh, Begam Hazrat Mahal flees to Nepal with her son Birjis Qadr.

4

Battle Sites

Battle of Chinhat: 30 June 1857

THE FIRST ENCOUNTER BETWEEN EAST India Company forces and those opposing the annexation of Awadh took place near Lucknow between the villages of Chinhat and Ismaelganj. The Company soldiers were led by Sir Henry Lawrence, the new chief commissioner. He had quickly reported on signs of 'dangerous coalitions' between sepoys already in the Company's army and men formerly in the king's army who had been recruited by the British into the new Oudh Irregular Force. Driving through Lucknow with two fellow officials, clods of earth were thrown at the men, and Lawrence reported this to the governor general as a sign of disaffection. In April, a meeting was held in the city between a grandson of the king of Delhi (the descendant of the Mughal emperors) and the Hindu Nana Sahib of Cawnpore to discuss the printing of a pamphlet calling on all citizens to prepare for a fight. An underground newspaper, *Payam-i-Azadi* (Message of Freedom), was produced, so revolutionary in tone that Lawrence closed down the press, banned the paper and decreed that anyone found with a copy might be executed. This collaboration was an indication that both Hindus and Muslims were prepared to unite and fight against the British.

On 1 May, men of the newly recruited 7th Oudh Irregular Infantry, stationed at the Mariaon cantonment north of Lucknow, refused greased cartridges for their rifles because they feared ritual contamination. Sepoys in Bengal had already refused to use them on the grounds that the grease came from pigs and cows, something which was not denied by army contractors. Two days later the same infantrymen sent a letter to the 48th Bengal Native Infantry stationed in and around Lucknow outlining a plot to murder their British officers. The letter was intercepted; Indian officers and men were arrested on the parade ground at Mariaon and stripped of their arms. Twenty of the mutineers were convicted, sentenced and hanged in front of the Macchi Bhawan fort. An 18-pounder gun loaded with grapeshot was placed on the main road, its wheels embedded in the earth, so it could not be hijacked by angry citizens. It was reported that 'The gallows, once erected, remained standing.' If the letter of 3 May had not been discovered, then Lucknow, not Meerut, would have seen the first outbreak of mutiny. The four soldiers who had intercepted the letter were rewarded for their loyalty by Lawrence himself at a reception held on the lawns of the small Residency at Mariaon. He presented the men, two officers and two sepoys, with swords, fine clothes and Rs 300 each (equivalent to over Rs 35,000 today or nearly £400).

Now, in the middle of May there was a spate of non-accidental fires in the cantonment and attempts to fire the officers' bungalows by shooting flaming arrows into the thatched roofs. Placards calling on Hindus and Muslims to rise up and kill the foreigners were secretly posted up at night in the city itself. By 25 May it was decided that the wives and children of British officers living in the cantonment should be accommodated in the main Residency in Lucknow.

These were the first refugees. At the same time taluqdars out in the countryside made attempts to take back land that had been lost in the Summary Settlement the previous year. Lawrence decided on a show of military force and sent officers and men from the 48th Native Infantry and 7th Light Cavalry towards Fatehgarh, the cantonment upriver from Cawnpore. However, on reaching the Ganges, about fifty men mutinied and set out for Delhi, where the mutineers from Meerut had established themselves three weeks earlier. Then came news of mutiny at Cawnpore itself, the major cantonment, and the force disintegrated with a number of British officers killed and some sepoys joining forces with Nana Sahib's men.

Here they learnt that British civilians, men, women and children had found shelter in what became known as Wheeler's Entrenchment, after the decision by Major General Sir Hugh Wheeler, commanding the Cawnpore troops, to defend a site containing two barracks. The entrenchment had a well, but that was the only thing in its favour. It was surrounded by a series of mud walls, some only three feet in

General Wheeler's Entrenchment at Cawnpore, 1858.
Felice Beato.

height. Although the dak (postal service) had ceased, messages were passed between Cawnpore and Lucknow, the former begging for help and the latter unable to provide it. Lawrence quickly realized that the Cawnpore entrenchment could not long withstand a siege and this led him to consider where Britons in Lucknow could find shelter should there be a local uprising. His first choice was the Macchi Bhawan, scene of the recent hangings of the mutineers. But he was outvoted by an ad hoc council of war, including engineers, who knew that the large masonry drains that honeycombed the hill underneath the old fort made it untenable. Indian mines would soon have been in place, ready to be detonated. Accommodation was cramped and confined in the fort, and the Residency doctor feared epidemic diseases like typhoid and cholera would spread rapidly. It was agreed that the city Residency should be prepared for a possible siege and large quantities of ammunition, food, alcohol and heavy guns were moved from the fort into the Residency. Lawrence seemed curiously reluctant to abandon the fort altogether, and a considerable amount of stores remained there. Guns that had been taken from the Residency were now moved back, and defensive works continued at Macchi Bhawan. Lawrence suffered a nervous collapse on 9 June from exhaustion, so a provisional council was formed that decided to release a large number of sepoys back to their villages, after they laid down their arms. In this way the remainder of the 7th Light Cavalry went, leaving behind only its native officers.

By 10 June contact had been lost between Lucknow and the newly created administrative divisions in Awadh. No more letters were received, nor messages from the commissioners and the deputy commissioners. Lawrence and his men knew when a division had been overrun because the post ceased to arrive. Salone, seventy miles south of Lucknow, was the last to go, when sepoys stationed here stopped obeying orders and told both the military and civilian officers to leave the station. Tellingly, as the British passed through the sepoys' quarters on their departure, some of the soldiers saluted them, while others were seen loading their muskets—there was still ambivalence among men who had served the Company for years. It was the same among Indian civilians—some, including friendly taluqdars, helped Britons escape to Benares and Allahabad, calculating that even though Delhi was presently in the hands of the rebels, ultimately the Company would win back control. It was a gamble.

Meanwhile those opposed to British rule, including many taluqdars and their private armies, were gathering at Nawabganj, a short, eighteen-mile ride east of Lucknow. News that Wheeler's Entrenchment at Cawnpore had surrendered to Nana Sahib's troops on 27 June undoubtedly emboldened the opposition in Awadh and at the same time produced a kind of desperation among the British gathered in Lucknow.

Chinhat today with a flyover on the Faizabad Road.
Anil Mehrotra.

On 29 June, an advance party of opposition forces gathered near the village of Chinhat, an old market for glazed pottery, as its name implies. Lawrence hesitated for twenty-four hours before confronting them, by which time the opposition had swelled to over 5,000 men and 800 cavalry. The following day a small Company force of around 750 officers and men assembled at dawn at the Iron Bridge in Lucknow. It included the Sikh cavalry armed with sabres. Troops then marched and rode to the bridge over the small Kukrail stream that bisected the Faizabad Road. Up to this point the road had been 'metalled', that is, covered with a firm surface of stone chippings mixed with tar. But beyond the Kukrail bridge there was only an embankment of loose, sandy soil, with gaps marked out for future drainage ditches. As the force advanced, its progress now slowed by the terrain, enemy guns started to fire from the fortified village of Ismaelganj to the left of the raised embankment, where the British were silhouetted against the skyline. Lawrence ordered the men to lie down and directed Lieutenant Bonham to fire the 8-inch howitzer. After an exchange of fire lasting twenty minutes, the enemy appeared to give way, but then regrouped and attacked from both sides of the embankment with a concentration of rebel infantry around Ismaelganj. The Company's ten artillery guns mounted on waggons were ordered to wheel across the embankment, from right to left, to face the village, but the steep banks and slippery, sandy soil meant this was a slow business and some of the waggons overturned. The Sikh cavalry, eighty-strong, under Captains Forbes and Hardinge, were then ordered to charge, but only two men went forward. The remainder turned their horses' heads and fled in the face of the enemy. Rebel infantry then launched a deadly fire so that it was impossible for the Company force to capture the village and a retreat was ordered. The elephant pulling the wooden limber for the howitzer panicked at the noise of the firing and ran off. An attempt to attach bullocks to the limber failed. Lieutenant Bonham was struck and the howitzer abandoned to the enemy. Seeing this, the drivers of the waggons carrying the guns and ammunition detached their horses and fled. The *bhistis* (water carriers) also deserted and men were left gasping with thirst in the heat and dust.

An elephant limber in Lucknow, 1858. Felice Beato.

Officers and men now had to fight their way eight miles back to the Residency, many on foot, with others clinging to the limbers or waggons. Cavalrymen took some foot soldiers up behind them on their horses, while others clung to the stirrups and were dragged along. Rebels were waiting for them at the Kukrail bridge but retreated when charged by Captain Radcliffe's small force of European volunteers. Men of HM 32nd Foot found their muskets would not fire and Captain Stevens of the regiment was wounded, sat down by the roadside and was overcome by rebels and killed. The Sikh cavalry, which had deserted, was rounded up, but fled again. The stricken force limped back to the Iron Bridge and re-entered the Macchi Bhawan and the Residency, from whence it had set out that morning.

The impact of the British defeat should not be underestimated nor overshadowed by the events that followed. A hundred and twelve Europeans had been killed, with forty-four wounded. Their burial places are unknown. Several officers were killed. The number of sepoys and men attached to the artillery limbers, waggons and ammunition carts was estimated at nearly two hundred killed, missing or deserted. In addition, the rebels were now in possession of the 8-inch howitzer, three of the field guns and nearly all the ammunition waggons.

Apart from the loss of life and weaponry, the fact that the British had lost this initial round, and lost quite spectacularly, gave the rebels confidence to continue the fight, and just as importantly, encouraged the sepoy regiments stationed in Lucknow to desert, which they did in large numbers. Infantrymen from the 4th and 7th Irregular regiments, who had been stationed at the Daulat Khana under Brigadier Gray, greeted the news of the Chinhat disaster with 'loud shouts, and commenced plundering the property of their officers ...' The brigadier and his officers were allowed to leave unharmed and fled to the Macchi Bhawan. Now only the old fort and the Residency remained in Company hands. The rest of the city had slipped out of British control. The kotwal (chief of police) was taken prisoner by the rebels and the city police, stationed in the Bara (Great) Imambara, joined the mutineers. Meanwhile the victorious rebels had arrived at the far side of the Gomti river, blocking both the Iron Bridge and the Stone Bridge. They quickly brought up their weapons including the captured 8-inch howitzer and began shelling the Residency.

Because the river was at its shallowest just before the monsoon, rebel cavalry were able to ford it lower down and were followed by the infantry. Guns were dragged across the river and by nightfall a substantial number of rebels had occupied the houses surrounding the Residency hill, knocked out some bricks to form loopholes and begun firing muskets direct into the Residency garrison. Indian workmen, women and children who had been handsomely paid to complete defensive works at the site now fled, together with domestic servants. 'Everything which was at the moment outside the line of works was lost,' reported Martin Gubbins, the financial commissioner.

The mistake in trying to maintain two garrisons—the Residency and the Macchi Bhawan—was immediately recognized. The latter was already low on food, gun ammunition, shot and shell. A local hand-operated telegraph on the Residency roof signalled a message on 1 July to Colonel Palmer at the fort: 'Spike the guns well, blow up the Fort and retire at midnight.' Heavy firing from the Residency began as a diversionary tactic and by 12.15 a.m. officers and men arrived at the Water Gate, with two 9-pounder guns and 'treasure' taken from the palaces. Lieutenant Thomas had laid a long, half-hour train to 240 barrels of gunpowder which ignited spectacularly at 12.30 a.m. However, it had not been possible to save a large amount of weaponry, including three 18-pounder guns, some 9-pounder guns with limbers, mortars, ammunition, percussion caps, stores and private property. The siege had begun.

The Siege: 30 June to 25 September 1857

Nearly 3,000 people were besieged on the Residency hill for four and a half months, unable to fight their way out and constantly bombarded by native forces surrounding the site. By the second and final relief in November 1857, approximately 1,500 people remained.

The exact figures are unknown because Indian soldiers and troops who had stayed loyal to the British were not counted, neither were Indian servants, nor many of the Anglo-Indian families who found a precarious shelter here. There were also six members of the Awadh and Mughal royal families, who had been arrested on charges of conspiring with the rebels and were now being held as hostages. None of the six was harmed during the siege because information on the rooms where they were held prisoner was immediately conveyed to the rebels outside who deliberately withheld their fire from that particular area. This demonstrated an acute knowledge by the opposition of what was going on inside the Residency garrison, a channel of information which was almost entirely one-way.

Mustafa Khan, elder brother of Wajid Ali Shah and one of the royal hostages held during the Residency siege. Getty Images.

Those within the complex knew little of what was going on in the city. The British were unaware, for example, that Birjis Qadr, son of the deposed king, had been crowned nominal head of the opposition in the Safed Barahdari (the White Pavilion) in the gardens of Qaisarbagh. When a 21-gun salute to mark the coronation was heard on 5 July, the day after Henry Lawrence's death, it was initially assumed that somehow British troops had miraculously arrived to relieve the Residency. The besieged also did not know that the leaders of the Sazman-Jawanan-e-Awadh had occupied the Mess House of the 32nd Regiment, the old Khurshid Manzil, while Maulvi Ahmadullah Shah's headquarters was established in the Tarawali Kothi. The Awadh court reassembled itself around the Qaisarbagh Palace and the new 'king', albeit only twelve years old, with his mother Begam Hazrat Mahal acted as regent. Further groups of supporters arrived in Lucknow including the Afridi Pathans from Malihabad, a long-established community of Afghan origin, and active recruitment for more soldiers began.

The White (Safed) Barahdari in Qaisarbagh, today.
Anil Mehrotra.

The question of surrender by the besieged British garrison has never been discussed, either in 1857 or today. Given that the opposition's plan was to force a surrender and humiliate the British, thus leading to annexation being reversed, it seems remarkable that no offer from the rebel side was recorded by either Indian or British historians. One explanation is that the victory at Chinhat seems to have taken the rebels by surprise as much as the British. Neither side was prepared for the outcome. Preparations for an expected siege of the Residency were not complete and a plan of action by the victors had not been worked out. Immediately after the British retreated in haste to the Residency on the evening of 30 June, disorder and looting broke out in the city by triumphant soldiers and supporters, many of whom came from rural backgrounds and were dazzled by their first sight of Lucknow and its riches. Sweet-shops were emptied first, then more serious looting took place, not just in the bazaars but from private houses too. This was one of the reasons for the 'coronation' of Birjis Qadr in order to head a revived government based on that of his father, which would reimpose law and order. By the time this had been partially implemented, the opportunity for a negotiated surrender by the British had passed. Yet it would not have been impossible in those early days. A guarantee of safe passage to Cawnpore could have been given in return for the twenty-three lakh of treasure newly buried in barrels under the Residency lawn. But after 25 July, when news of the massacre of British women and children at the Bibighar in Cawnpore was related to horrified listeners in the garrison, there was no surrender or even talk of it. To surrender was to die.

Because the electric telegraph with its receiving and transmitting office in the Residency's former Banqueting Hall had been cut, communication could only be by letters smuggled in and out, or verbal messages. A brief report by Gujral Brahmin visiting Lucknow soon after the siege began spoke of the plunder by rebel sepoys, some of whom returned to their villages with their loot. He also estimated that at first as many as a hundred mutineers were killed daily by accurate firing from the Residency. If the dead soldiers were Hindus and had relatives nearby, their bodies were cremated, but for those from outlying villages, their corpses were simply thrown into the river. The Muslim dead were buried in common graves. Brahmin also reported that the rebels, whom he called mutineers, had taken over the gardens of Lucknow's inhabitants to pitch their tents. No shortage of food was reported and shops remained open, but there seemed to be a lack of ready ammunition and searches were being made for saltpetre so more gunpowder could be manufactured. Entrenchments in the city were allocated to various taluqdars and their private armies to defend. Raja Man Singh, for example, who vacillated in his support between the begam and the British, was put in charge of the Sher Darwaza and adjoining stables with his 7,000 men.

On 2 July, less than two days into the siege, Henry Lawrence was mortally wounded by a shell from the 8-inch howitzer, captured by the enemy at Chinhat and fired into the Residency. He immediately appointed Major Banks to succeed him as chief commissioner and Colonel Inglis to command the troops in the Residency garrison. Major J. Anderson was in command of the artillery and engineering operations. Lawrence died on the morning of 4 July. The following day the annual monsoon began, although it did little to counteract the 'excessive heat' noted by those who kept diaries during the siege. A number of books based on these diaries were subsequently published, the first as early as February 1858, even before Lucknow had been recaptured. It is easy to conjure up from these accounts the incessant noise of constant firing from both sides, the mad stampedes through the site of horses and bullocks left without food, the smell of putrefaction from dead animals and the trauma of seeing fellow human beings killed daily, sometimes by decapitation from a well-

Dr Fayrer's house in the Residency where Sir Henry Lawrence died on 4 July 1857. Author's collection.

placed round shot. Babies and young children sickened and died, food was generally in short supply, tobacco had run out because no-one had thought to bring in supplies, clothing could not be replaced, servants deserted and the loyalty of the sepoys who remained in the garrison was a constant worry. We will not follow the day-to-day privations of the majority of the besieged, which have been amply recorded, but will concentrate on the military aspect of the first stage of the siege which began immediately after the defeat at Chinhat.

Those who found themselves suddenly under siege took a few days to evaluate their position. Two months had passed since the first signs of mutiny in the Lucknow cantonments at the beginning of May. There had been warnings of trouble from sepoys loyal to their British officers. Now news of the mutinies at Meerut, Delhi and Cawnpore clearly and horribly demonstrated that the East India Company, in northern India at least, was under the most serious threat in its 250-year existence. Without giving the appearance of alarm, Lawrence had steadily been preparing for the worst. The hill on which the garrison stood was for the first time in its history examined to see where gun batteries could be placed. Martin Gubbins got a wall built around his two-storey house and a six-foot-high semicircle of logs embedded in tamped earth was erected in front of the portico of the Residency itself. A new tower was started on the city side of the Macchi Bhawan and here it was not possible to conceal what was being built because 300 labourers were at work daily. It had been hoped that all preparations would be completed before trouble actually started but the defeat at Chinhat precipitated the siege. For several days the commissariat that dealt with army supplies was unable to operate. People and animals went hungry and some who had intended to enter the complex were inadvertently shut out while others, mainly native servants who were inside, deserted. 'Although they could not get in, they succeeded in getting out,' reported Captain Wilson dryly.

Inside the complex were the following military units in varying numbers:

General Staff
Brigade Staff
Artillery
Engineers
7th Regiment Light Cavalry
HM 32nd Foot
Detachment of HM 84th Foot
13th Regiment Native Infantry
41st Regiment Native Infantry
48th Regiment Native Infantry
71st Regiment Native Infantry
Oude Irregular Force
Officers not attached to the Oude Brigade

In addition there were a number of civilian volunteers.

The Residency compound, developed over the previous seventy years, was an ad hoc mix of residential, military, official, financial and religious buildings, which included barracks, stables, a treasury, a hamam (bath), a banqueting hall, bungalows, a mosque and a mazar (Muslim shrine), a church and an infants' school, as well as the main Residency itself. The site sloped sharply towards the river on its north-eastern flank. This was relatively easy to defend with a redan battery that could monitor the Iron Bridge and Captain Bazaar, a double row of one-storey shops on the riverbank. To the west Innes's garrison commanded a small stream that ran from the river with a road running parallel. It was the south-eastern quarter, the military area with its barracks, Brigade Mess and Sikh cavalry stables, which was the most vulnerable, because the hill levelled off here and only a narrow road separated it from the houses outside. These were tall buildings clustered around the foot of the hill, and occupied by the Anglo-Armenian traders Johannes & Son and their shop. The busy Cawnpore Road skirted the site and there were several mosques here, whose minaret towers provided unique vantage points for snipers.

Military action by the British trapped in the Residency complex during the first twelve weeks of the siege was almost entirely reactive, and defensive rather than offensive. The first sortie was made on 7 July against the rebel marksmen in Johannes's House who were firing down into the Residency. A party of eighty men from the garrison, accompanied by engineers, made a hole in the wall enclosing the compound and blew open the door to the house. They found the enemy inside, including a large number of Pasi, an aboriginal tribe who were particularly skilled with the bow and arrow. Whether they had been recruited by rebel leaders or whether they were protesting against Company rule is unknown. No one spoke for these illiterate

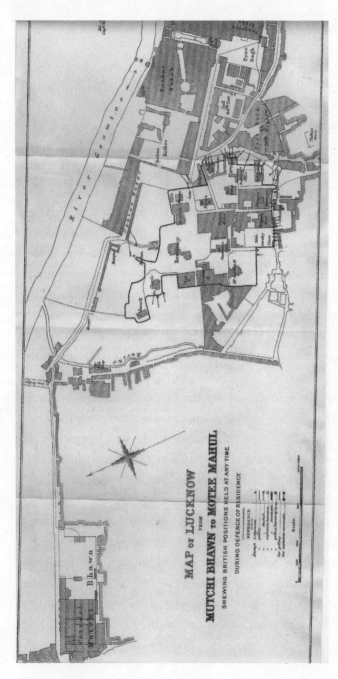

'Map of Lucknow from Mutchi Bhawn to Motee Mahul shewing British positions held at any time during defence of Residency'. Edinburgh and London: W. & A.K. Johnston. Scale 1,200 feet to 3 inches. Map size 26½ x 8 inches.

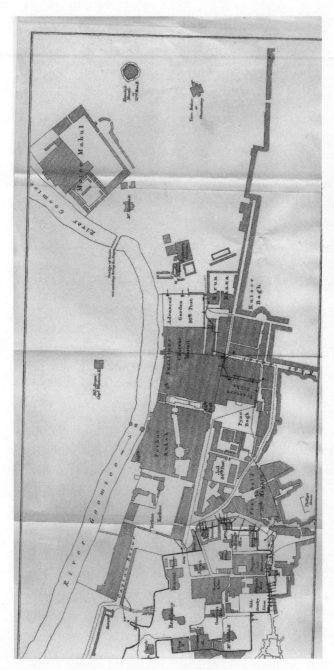

'Map of Lucknow from Mutchi Bhawn to Motee Mahul shewing British positions held at any time during defence of Residency'. Edinburgh and London: W. & A.K. Johnston. Scale 1,200 feet to 3 inches. Map size 26½ x 8 inches.

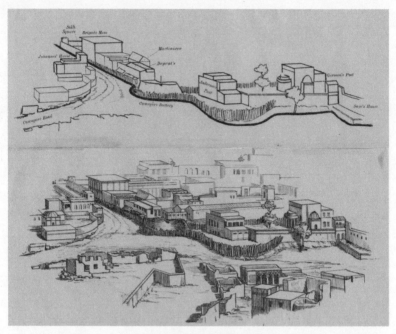

The vulnerable Cawnpore battery in the Residency. Note the proximity
of Johannes's House. *Lucknow and Oudh in the Mutiny*, Lieutenant-
General McLeod Innes, 1895.

people but it illustrates the wide-ranging nature of the opposition
faced by the British. Johannes's House was cleared, most of the rebels
fleeing, leaving twenty of their dead behind. Unwisely the sortie
party then withdrew to the Residency garrison without blowing up
the house itself, which was soon reoccupied by rebel marksmen and
archers.

Batteries were quickly erected by the opposition around the
Residency hill, some within sixty yards of the site. They were made
from teak rafters and doors plucked from houses and embedded
upright in the ground to form a wooden wall. A bank of earth was
piled up on either side as support and a square hole, or embrasure,

left at intervals for a gun muzzle to be inserted. Because the rebel offensives took place immediately outside the Residency, sophisticated street-fighting tactics were employed that were previously unknown. Deep trenches were dug across the streets, handy missiles of brick and timber collected in convenient piles, screens of wooden palisades embedded in banks of earth to act as shields for buildings and the skilful deployment of guns. Gubbins reported: 'Sometimes they kept their gun concealed behind the corner of a building, ran out, fired, and immediately retired before we could return the shot, pulling back the gun with a drag rope. In other places the gun was kept at the bottom of an inclined plane, dragged to the top to be fired and then let the recoil force it back down.' When shells were fired from the Residency at these rebel guns, the Indian gunners had time to jump into trenches dug near their own batteries. In these first encounters and even more so when the relief forces arrived, they prefigured fighting during the Paris Commune thirteen years later and mark a distinct shift away from the old patterns of medieval warfare that were still in force a few decades earlier, like the siege of Bharatpur in 1825, for example.

The shortage of rebel ammunition, reported by Brahmin at the start of the siege, evidently continued and improvisations were made by firing logs of wood bound with iron into the garrison. The destroyed electric telegraph along the Cawnpore Road now provided a handy supply of wooden posts and copper wire which could also be used. British officers noted that their own fired cannonballs were immediately picked up by the enemy and returned, and shots were interchanged several times between the combatants in a grisly game of tennis. Palisades were quickly improvised in the Residency and when the supply of rafters was exhausted, walls of canvas tent material were put up, which offered no protection of course but meant that the enemy could not see what was behind them. Anything substantial that could be utilized was dragged in to reinforce the barricades, including carriages, furniture and even a harp case. Windows in the Residency and other houses were barricaded with large bookcases and wardrobes.

One reason the Macchi Bhawan had been abandoned was the fear of its being undermined, but this now began around the Residency hill. Tunnels, or galleries as they were called, were excavated, barrels of gunpowder placed at the far end and exploded. The skill lay in directing the tunnel to reach under a significant building, which could then be demolished. One enemy mine exploded inside the Water Gate, which was followed by a prolonged attack on the redan battery and Innes's garrison where rebels tried to plant scaling ladders against the makeshift barricades, but were knocked down. Further galleries were started around the perimeter and the sounds of rebel workmen digging away was detected by a handful of Cornishmen of the 32nd Foot, themselves former tin miners. One gallery, started in a native house nearby, was interrupted when Company engineers sank their own shaft into it, lowered barrels of gunpowder and blew the whole thing up, including the house. But other enemy mines went undetected and, when exploded, brought down parts of two houses along the vulnerable south-eastern quarter. Hand grenades were thrown down on to the rebels attempting to climb into the area. Meanwhile a 24-pounder enemy gun fired from outside the western boundary into the compound hit the church, Innes's garrison and the Residency itself, bringing down the north-east wing and killing four men who got buried under the falling rubble. Heavy cannons like these had a considerable range but at the same time there was hand-to-hand fighting when rebels got into the financial garrison building inside the Baillie Guard gate and began pulling at the bayonets protruding through loopholes. Only the explosion of a mine under a brick building that collapsed on to opposition forces saved the situation.

'Lying in wait': Bengal engineer in a gallery, listening for counter-mining. *Sketches and Incidents of the siege of Lucknow from Drawings made during the Siege*, Clifford Henry Mecham, 1858.

On 18 August, a rebel mine exploded under the Sikh Square, killing seven men and causing a 30-foot breach in the barricades and revealing the houses opposite filled with the enemy. Somehow the breach was patched up with doors and planks torn from the buildings in the Residency. Johannes's House, where much of the firing had come from, and his shop, were finally demolished at the end of August by a sortie from the Residency carrying four barrels of gunpowder. The explosion dislodged a large quantity of wood, including rafters and doors that were immediately seized to infill the barricades. An attempt was made to burn the Baillie Guard entrance when rebels piled up combustible material and wood outside the gates. The fire was extinguished and new loopholes made in the side walls. It was reported that the main Residency building was 'so pierced with roundshot that it was little better than a sieve'.

Brigadier Inglis, who was now in command of both the military and civilians after the death of Major Banks, the acting chief commissioner, assessed the situation frankly. He knew it was impossible for the besieged garrison to fight its way out: 'I have more than 120 sick and wounded, at least 220 women and about 230 children and no carriage [transport].' There were 350 European men and about 300 natives, plus twenty-three lakh of treasure buried under the Residency lawn and thirty guns. Help was promised by General Havelock in Cawnpore, but he was waiting for reinforcements which could take three to four weeks to arrive. Meanwhile the rebel shelling continued with a 32-pounder gun brought up to the Clock Tower, directly in front of the Baillie Guard gate, which somehow resisted destruction. The chief engineer, Captain Fulton, was killed, beheaded by a cannonball. The number of rebel matchlockmen carrying old-fashioned muskets increased when the taluqdar Raja Man Singh arrived with his own troops. Constant firing had demolished the Brigade Mess and Innes's garrison and it was later reported that there was 'not an exterior building along our whole line of defence which did not exhibit the marks of excessive dilapidation'. Lieutenant James Graham of the Light Cavalry shot himself due to a 'temporary aberration of mind', a tactful way of explaining his suicide.

It was, therefore, with extreme relief that the distant sound of artillery fire was heard coming from the Cawnpore direction on 23 September. Two days later, numbers of people from the city were seen streaming across the two bridges with bundles of possessions on their heads. Sepoys, matchlockmen and cavalry crossed the river, some swimming across. It was the end of the beginning, but there was still a long way to go.

Baillie Guard gate, 1858. Felice Beato.

First Relief of Lucknow: 25 September 1857

Within a couple of months of the annexation of Awadh in February 1856, the chief commissioner (formerly the British Resident) Sir James Outram had returned to England on sick leave. After a year's recuperation, he was appointed to lead an expeditionary force during the Anglo-Persian War, for which he got the rank of lieutenant-general. But as the scale and speed of the revolt in India became clear, he was hurriedly recalled and returned to Calcutta on 31 July 1857. He was appointed to command the divisions of Dinapore and Cawnpore and although this was a military appointment, Outram chose to act as a 'civilian volunteer' under the commander-in-chief, Sir Colin Campbell. This was an altruistic and generous gesture on Outram's part so that he would not be seen to upstage the older Brigadier-General Sir Henry Havelock, who had made three

Sir James Outram, painting by Thomas Brigstocke.

unsuccessful attempts to reach Lucknow and relieve the Residency.
Each time Havelock was forced back to Cawnpore, where his field
force eventually was reduced to 700 men, due mainly to cholera.
He was also threatened by the rebel Gwalior Contingent pushing
up from central India and led by Tantia Topi (or Tope), one of Nana
Sahib's officers. Topi's aim was to recapture Cawnpore for his master.

Lord Canning, the governor general, was insistent that Lucknow
took priority even if it meant abandoning Cawnpore to the rebels.
He said that the political importance of Cawnpore was 'not to be
weighed against the relief of Lucknow'. So, HM 90th Regiment and
the 5th Fusiliers were sent up to Cawnpore from Allahabad by river
steamer and were joined by men of the 64th and 84th Regiments.
Another eighty-nine men came from Benares and Brigadier-General
James Neill was already in Cawnpore with his 1st Madras Fusiliers. By
18 September engineers had laid a floating bridge across the Ganges

into Awadh, and Havelock's force, now with reinforcements, crossed the river for the fourth time that summer.

General Sir Henry Havelock's statue in Trafalgar Square, London, by William Behnes, 1861.

Rapidly advancing towards Lucknow, Havelock found a large rebel troop, estimated at some 10,000 men, clustered at Alambagh, a recently built palatial house on the outskirts of the city. The rebels were chased towards Charbagh bridge, the only crossing over the Haider canal that bordered the southern approach to Lucknow. Alambagh was to become the British headquarters for the next six months and its strategic importance, on the road to Cawnpore, cannot be underestimated. But now, on 24 September, Havelock's force enjoyed a day's rest and the chance to dry their clothes, sodden during the last monsoon downpours. News arrived through a series of harkaras (messengers) that Delhi had been recaptured by the British. This undoubtedly gave everyone a boost. Meanwhile rebel soldiers had crept silently and unseen through surrounding jungle and two 9-pounder guns concealed in trees at the Charbagh bridge opened fire.

Plans were made for the following day, 25 September, and the entry into Lucknow. Wounded men and baggage were to remain at Alambagh for the moment with the 78th Regiment ('the Highlanders') while the rest of the force, once across the bridge, were to veer right along the canal path, make a wide half circle to the east of the city, then turn sharply west through the palaces that lined the riverbank and approach the Residency. This route avoided the main Hazratganj Road that ran through the centre of 'new' Lucknow, developed during the previous half century. Accounts differ on how the heavily defended Charbagh bridge was crossed, although General Havelock's son, Lieutenant Henry (Harry) Havelock was one of the first across, with Colonel Fraser Tytler. The two riders were followed by other horsemen who leapt across the earthen barricade erected by the rebels at the city end of the bridge and bayoneted the gunners crouching in a battery, or defensive trench. The canal was the dividing line between the rural outskirts of jungle and planted fields and the city proper with tall houses and narrow high-walled lanes. Captain Olpherts charged a group of rebel gunners, seized their two guns, attached them to his own spare limbers and rode on triumphantly, all under heavy crossfire. He was awarded the VC (Victoria Cross).

Fight on Charbagh bridge. Getty Images.

The unpaved roads were a sea of mud. Men, ankle-deep in slush, dragged heavy guns over soggy ground where the wheels of the limbers sank into deep ruts. Gradually the main body of troops wheeled round the outskirts of the city, then through a narrow passage that led to one of the riverside palaces, the Chattar Manzil, where the men waited for the Highlanders to arrive. Enemy firing came from the large Qaisarbagh Palace and annoyingly from the Khurshid Manzil, now the headquarters of the opposition's military junta. The Highlanders had been instructed to hold the Charbagh bridge until the major part of the force and the baggage train had cleared it, which they did under heavy fire for several hours. Then, instead of following the semicircular route to the Chattar Manzil, the rendezvous point, they mistook the road, it is said, and plunged into Hazratganj, where they met a hail of bullets from the loopholed houses lining the broad street. Fighting on, the Highlanders were able to overrun a battery in front of the Qaisarbagh Palace before sighting Outram and Havelock 500 yards in front of the Baillie Guard entrance to the Residency. But there was still a long way to go. By now, night was falling. Outram, who was of course familiar with the area from his time as Resident and then commissioner, wanted to pause to let the Highlanders, the rearguard, the heavy guns, the baggage train and the wounded catch up so they were all together. There was a discussion over whether to enter the Residency that night, or camp nearby and go in the following day, 26 September. Brigadier James Neill was shot and killed under an archway while waiting for the guns to be brought up.

'Neill Darwaza', the Qaisarbagh gateway where Brigadier-General James Neill was killed on 25 September 1857. Photographed in 1858 by Felice Beato.

Neill Darwaza today. Anil Mehrotra.

It is clear that in the darkness there was confusion among different parts of the large force, strung out in unfamiliar territory and under fire. The Highlanders again took a turn along the Khas Bazaar, the shopping area, and were again under heavy fire from the houses above the shops. Lieutenant William Moorsom, who had been detailed to survey the city immediately after annexation, had luckily brought some rough copies of his survey with him and he was able to guide Havelock along the Clock Tower road that led directly to the Residency entrance, in spite of deep trenches having been cut across the road. Other groups of exhausted men bivouacked where they could, sinking down in buildings outside the Residency. A group was stranded outside the Moti Mahal Palace and had to be rescued the next day when dawn broke. Firing continued from enemy troops across the river. It was by no means the happy or definitive relief that Canning had wanted. Those who stood outside the Baillie Guard gate and shouted could hear the barricade behind the gate being removed

'The road by which Sir Henry Havelock entered the Residency', 1858.
Felice Beato.

before they could be let in. Fighting continued during the night and
the next day and a number of wounded troops in *doolies* (palanquins)
were massacred where they lay, waiting for a rescue that didn't come.
It was discovered that the rebels had manufactured an ingenious
bullet-proof screen which could be wheeled into place to block off
entrances to buildings. On 26 September Captain Bazaar, the row
of small shops below the Residency, was cleared of rebel sepoys who
were chased into the Gomti and shot or drowned. Three large rebel
guns were captured, one of which was dragged to safety by Private
Duffy, for which he was awarded a VC. Engineers working under
Colonel Robert Napier were able to open up a direct route between
the Chattar Manzil and the Residency through the use of explosives,
which allowed the guns to be brought safely in.

On 30 September, Havelock provided the returns of dead
and wounded. Over 1,000 officers and men had been killed, and

others wounded since the departure from Alambagh at dawn on 25 September. And 207 officers and men had died on the march from Cawnpore. It was a heavy price to pay.

The Blockade: 26 September to 17 November 1857

James Outram took overall command on 26 September, retaining Brigadier Inglis in command of the garrison. There were now more than 2,000 extra men and Outram deployed them immediately in clearing and occupying the riverbank palaces to provide for their accommodation. General Havelock moved into the house of the judicial commissioner, Manaton Ommaney, who had been killed. Sorties were sent out at dawn to destroy the enemy batteries immediately outside the Residency garrison, including one opposite the vulnerable south-east perimeter. Facing heavy musket fire, the troops fought house to house along the barricaded and loopholed lanes and were able to blow up three large buildings, clearing a range of about 300 yards. The party was back in the Residency by 9 a.m. A further sortie to try to secure the Iron Bridge was unsuccessful, although the 24-pounder gun which had done such damage to the Residency and the church was taken and destroyed. Outram had hoped that by capturing the Iron Bridge supplies and food could be brought into the garrison, but this had proved impossible.

Both Outram and Havelock had initially thought that the garrison was facing starvation and that an immediate evacuation would be possible. As a result, they had not brought any supplies with them, although Alambagh was now well stocked with essentials including rum, spirits, wine, tea, coffee, sugar and tobacco. Outram's instructions from Lord Canning had been to bring out the women and children as a priority, followed by the sick and wounded. This meant evacuating 1,500 vulnerable people and Outram realized this was not feasible given the heavy loss of life as the relieving force had fought their way in. 'Want of carriages alone rendered the transport through five miles of disputed suburb an impossibility,' he said. He faced two choices, neither very promising. He could leave a token force of 300 men at the Residency garrison and try to cut his way through to the safety of Alambagh with the larger body of troops shielding the defenceless evacuees. But 300 men would not be sufficient to hold the garrison against an active opposition, or to prevent the rebels from recapturing the positions so dearly won during the previous week. The alternative was to stay put until further military help could arrive but to ration food supplies more strictly. He decided on the latter plan, at the same time continuing to send sorties out along the Cawnpore Road to drive back the rebels. This involved both street fighting and, at the same time, the demolition of the houses that lined the road. Gates and doors had been bricked up by those occupying the buildings. There were narrow lanes, high garden walls and continual sniper fire. But engineer-led troops, working through house after house with crowbars and pickaxes, were able to capture the principal buildings along the road and blow them up. The house belonging to a civilian, Mr Phillips, was reached and occupied and its extensive garden became a permanent and useful outpost. Men of the 78th Regiment moved in to 'comfortable accommodation' and at the same time were able to protect a large section of the entrenchment surrounding the garrison and open a passageway to the now secured river palaces. This did not take place without some opposition. Mining continued to be a threat and there was some rebel firing from the roof of the jail that was awkwardly situated near Phillips's garden and the palaces. Nevertheless, the position was held.

On 6 October, Outram discovered that the amount of food in the garrison had been underestimated and that there was in fact enough to enable it to hold out for several more weeks with judicious rationing. In the confusion at the beginning of the siege the commissariat had not kept proper accounts of supplies brought into the site. But ammunition for the new Enfield rifles that the 2,000 extra men were carrying was in short supply, because they had not expected to spend much time in the city. There were plenty of musket ball cartridges but these were useless for the Enfields. With some ingenuity, two officers set up a 'manufactory' in the Treasury. Lieutenant Sewell had a mould for casting and Major North of the 60th Rifles had learnt how to manufacture rifle cartridges. A dozen Indian men in the garrison were taught and soon cartridges 'as neat and good as those served out to the army' were being produced. Meanwhile mining and countermining continued and the British were losing ground. Their picquet (a temporary military outpost) overlooking two major bazaars was blown up although the enemy were said to have lost 450 men during the action. Evidence of the rebels' skill at mining came when galleries were found under the river palaces, and three mines exploded here. The aftermath of an exploded mine under the Chattar Manzil Palace was caught on camera showing massive chunks of fallen masonry, rafters and rubble. But the river palaces, which were to act as the eventual escape route, were successfully held though they were closely, almost intimately, connected with the city's other buildings through a maze of passages and courtyards. Loopholes were made in adjoining buildings within thirty yards of the British-occupied palaces. Zigzag trenches or saps dug in front of Innes's garrison had allowed troops to secure the city end of the Iron Bridge. With the capture of their batteries, the opposition adopted new tactics. The remaining guns were pulled back and no longer used to batter the defences but to fire directly into the garrison. This led to numerous casualties when round shot, bullets and an 18-pounder cannonball came crashing into residential accommodation. Attempts to storm the defences had ceased in favour of killing those enclosed within. Food rations were reduced again.

Meanwhile, the detachment of British troops left at the Alambagh Palace, south of the city, was being strengthened. The road to Cawnpore, on which the palace lay, was open and along it came commissariat stores, cattle, fodder, food supplies, men and weapons. The telegraph line to Cawnpore had been reinstated. By the end of October, nearly 1,000 armed men had arrived, forerunners to the troops that would accompany Sir Colin Campbell on the second, successful relief of Lucknow.

Restored electric telegraph along the Cawnpore Road, 1858. Felice Beato.

Second Relief of Lucknow: 14 to 22 November 1857

Sir Colin Campbell assumed command of the Indian Army on 17 August 1857 on his arrival in Calcutta from England. He was sixty-five years old and had retired after a distinguished military career, but was now called on for service again. He arrived in Cawnpore at the beginning of November and left on the 9th for Lucknow, arriving at the Alambagh Palace outpost on the 12th with a force of 4,500. Here he met Thomas Kavanagh, a civilian clerk who had attached himself to the garrison as an assistant field engineer. Kavanagh had volunteered to walk the four miles between the Residency and Alambagh disguised as an Indian and guided by a local man, Misr Kanouji Lal. They were able to give Campbell a code of signals from Outram to be used to communicate with the garrison. Kavanagh, an Irishman, and not an Anglo-Indian as some thought, was subsequently awarded the VC, one of only five civilians to receive it. A signal flag was hoisted from Alambagh to mark his safe arrival.

Thomas Kavanagh, 1858. Felice Beato.

Misr Kanouji Lal, Kavanagh's guide. Photographer unknown.

It was possible from the Residency tower to see the Union flag flying from the top of Alambagh. Although the distance between the two was considerable, a glance at the map shows the two buildings were almost directly aligned, Alambagh being due south of the Residency. The intervening space was covered by 'dense city' as the British called it, brick buildings one or two storeys high and beyond the canal were fields. Standing on a hill, as the Residency did, it was quite feasible, with a good telescope, to see Alambagh, standing on another slight prominence in the middle of fields. This suggested to Martin Gubbins that it should be possible to set up a semaphore between the two buildings. In the best *Boy's Own* tradition, Gubbins looked up 'telegraph' in the *Penny Cyclopaedia* from his library and erected a semaphore on one of the Residency's two towers, while men at Alambagh did the same. Campbell's arrival on 12 November was announced to the Residency by telegraph and followed by news of his planned advance into the city. From the garrison preparations were made to facilitate the entry of Campbell's troops. A battery for heavy guns was built in the garden of Phillips's House, which was surrounded by a high wall. The wall was to be blown up the moment the relief force entered the Cawnpore Road, revealing the guns.

Lithograph (from a photograph?) taken from the roof of the Residency showing distant buildings including the Martinière.

Campbell's plan was not to force an entry across the narrow
Charbagh bridge over the canal, the pinch-point into the city, as
Havelock had done, but to extend his base south-east of the canal
and then swing round. He and his men set out at daybreak on 13
November and the force first had to deal with the sturdy mud-brick
fort of Jallalabad, built by an earlier nawab and lying south of the city.
Enough of it was blown up to make it indefensible, although it never
played a major part in the conflict. Campbell was joined that night
by reinforcements from Cawnpore and his troop now numbered
about 600 cavalry and 3,500 infantrymen together with the artillery,
engineers and sailors from the Naval Brigade. The following day the
main column marched due east from Alambagh towards the Dilkusha
Palace, a pleasant building in a well-stocked deer park, which had
been modelled on Seaton Delaval Hall, a country house in England.
Rebels occupying the house and its detached kitchen and stable
buildings were taken by surprise as Campbell had previously sent
reconnaissance parties to Charbagh to lay a false trail.

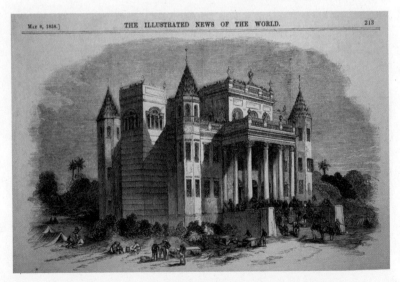

Dilkusha, from *The Illustrated News of the World*, 1858.

A breach was made in the high brick wall surrounding the park and men of the 93rd Regiment marched through it in a double column and lined up inside. An enemy battery concealed behind the palace opened fire but was silenced by the artillery. Ten men of the regiment had been killed or wounded, but the Dilkusha was captured and the semaphore quickly erected on the roof signalled the news to the Residency. Crossing the park, the soldiers moved on to the Martinière School, a large fantastical building erected at the end of the eighteenth century by Major-General Claude Martin of the East India Company. Although designed as a highly defensible structure (which made it attractive to Campbell), its pupils and masters had reluctantly sought refuge in the Residency and were allocated buildings in the south-east military quarter. Their school was quickly cleared of its rebel occupiers and those who were not bayoneted were chased into the adjoining river. The semaphore on the Dilkusha was dismantled and re-erected at the top of the Martinière.

But the anticipated advance into the city had to be postponed for a day because provisions and ammunition had not arrived, so the men bivouacked at the Martinière. What baggage they had was stored in the Dilkusha and an enemy attack on the house was beaten off by a detachment of horse artillery and cavalry. That evening, 15 November, Campbell semaphored to Outram and Havelock in the Residency: 'Advance tomorrow'. Lieutenant Roberts, who later rose to become Field Marshal Lord Roberts VC, was sent back to Alambagh with 150 camels and some cavalry, to collect the missing ammunition which he delivered to an anxious Campbell, standing on the steps of the Martinière. It was near here that Lieutenant Augustus Mayne of the Bengal Horse Artillery was killed by a sadhu (holy man) who suddenly pulled out a pistol from under his leopard skin and shot the young officer dead. Mayne was buried the following day, close to where he had fallen, 'in his blue frock-coat and long boots' with his monocle in place 'as he always wore it in the heat of the fray'. His grave lies today at the side of the Martinière golf course.

The Martinière, 1858. Felice Beato.

The troops were issued with rations for three days and marched forward at 8 a.m. on 16 November after an address by Campbell. The advance column was directed by Thomas Kavanagh and Misr Kanouji Lal, and the troops were able to cross the Haider canal without getting their feet or hooves wet. The rebels, anticipating that Campbell would attempt the Charbagh bridge route again, had not only destroyed the bridge, but had dammed the canal to produce a deep water barricade where the bridge had stood. This led to the eastern end of the canal, which because of its original faulty construction had always ridden higher than the river, becoming completely dry. The canal walls here were also broken down so it was possible for the entire force not only to cross with ease, but to drag their heavy guns with them too. Continuing north on the west bank of the river, through narrow lanes and fields enclosed with mud walls, the troops swung sharply left towards the Sikanderbagh, a square high-walled garden with a two-storeyed summer house at its centre, a wooden pavilion in front and an elaborate gatehouse. Bastions stood at each corner and the walls had been loopholed. Here the troops divided, with three companies of the 93rd moving south to capture the Chaupar Stables near Hazratganj. The remaining men and heavy artillery arrived at Sikanderbagh under musket fire from neighbouring houses.

Sikanderbagh gateway today. Anil Mehrotra.

VCs and statues

The largest number of VCs (Victoria Crosses), ever won in a single day was at Lucknow on 16 November 1857 during the second, successful relief of the besieged Residency. This was when Colin Campbell's force was pushing towards the Residency from the east, capturing Sikanderbagh and Shah Najaf. For a full list see:

https://en.wikipedia.org/wiki/List_of_Indian_Mutiny_Victoria_Cross_recipients

Not surprisingly many statues were erected in India and Britain to the British heroes of the Uprising:

Lousada Barrow, later Major-General, who served under Havelock and Outram, and was present at the recapture of Lucknow in March 1858, was commemorated wearing civilian dress in a rather poor marble statue now in the State Museum, Lucknow.

Sir Colin Campbell (later Lord Clyde) stands in George Square, Glasgow, his sola topi clasped in his right hand and his left resting on a fallen palm tree, clutching a telescope and a sword.

Major-General Sir Henry Havelock stands on a plinth in Trafalgar Square, London, embodied in a fine bronze by the sculptor William Behnes. It was erected by public subscription in 1861.

Brigadier-General James Neill was commemorated with a bronze statue, funded by public subscription, erected in Madras (now Chennai) in 1860. It was removed in 1937 and placed in the Madras Museum.

Lieutenant-General Sir James Outram's bronze equestrian statue was relocated to the gardens of the Victoria Memorial Hall, Calcutta, and there are further statues of him in Westminster Abbey, St Paul's Cathedral and the Victoria Embankment, all in London.

Sir James Outram's statue by John Henry Foley, Victoria Memorial gardens, Calcutta.

Sir William Peel, Commander of HMS *Shannon,* which assisted with its sailors and 68-pounder guns in the recapture, was commemorated in a statue that stood in Eden Gardens, Calcutta, but which was subsequently moved to Barrackpore.

There is no statue of Begam Hazrat Mahal in Lucknow. When one was proposed after Independence, a number of conservative Muslims were against the idea of erecting a statue to a Muslim woman in a public place. A marble statue of a seated Queen Victoria under an elaborate canopy had been erected in a park near the Residency and when this was removed to the State Museum, a plaque to Hazrat Mahal was put in its place and the park renamed after her.

The army commandant Raja Jai Lal Singh is commemorated with a statue and inscription in the Amar Shahid Raja Jai Lal Singh Park at the western end of Hazratganj, where he was hanged. A statue to the heroine of Sikanderbagh, the unnamed African soldier who shot British troops, has morphed over the years into the bust of a Dalit woman.

It is clear that earth embankments had been constructed around the garden. British accounts mention high banks but these were not natural formations. What has never been answered is why 2,000 of the opposition allowed themselves to be trapped inside the Sikanderbagh walls from which there was no escape. Only Lieutenant Roberts has a partial explanation. 'The rebels, never dreaming that we should stop to attack such a formidable position, had collected in the Sikanderbagh with the intention of falling upon our right flank so soon as we should become entangled amongst the streets and houses of the Hazratganj.' It was a terrible miscalculation on the part of the opposition. Because the main gateway was barred from inside, British heavy artillery began to pound the south-eastern bastion of the garden walls and after thirty minutes a breach approximately three feet square was made in it. Arguments over who was first through the breach (and indeed where the breach was) continued until the end of the nineteenth century with men from

Sikanderbagh wall today, showing likely area of the breach.
Anil Mehrotra.

the 4th Punjab Infantry, the 53rd and the 93rd regiments claiming
the honour. Roberts tactfully says 'Highlanders and Sikhs, Punjabi
Mahomedans, Dogras and Pathans, all vied with each other in the
generous competition.' A further error by the opposition was made
when the main gate was opened to let in some stragglers but the
attempt to close it was foiled by Mukarrah Khan of the 4th Punjab
Infantry and the troops poured in. Rebels inside fought bravely, first
with muskets and when their ammunition was finished, 'hurled the
muskets amongst us like javelins, bayonets first', then used their
swords, slashing at the troops' legs. About a hundred British and
Company troops were killed, but less than a handful of the 2,000
rebels escaped. It was later found that many of them had belonged
to the 71st Native Infantry, which had been stationed at the
Mariaon cantonment. They had been told to go on home leave in
May until the trouble was over, and a number of the Sikanderbagh
corpses, shovelled into the trenches outside, still carried their leave

certificates. Other dead soldiers were from the 11th Oude Irregular Infantry, and strange as it may seem, both mutinous regiments were still using their English colours (flags) and observing the English discipline of muster rolls. Of the reformed regiments from the king's disbanded army, the Nadri and Tirchha were prominent here with their green silk flags. British and Company troops who had fallen were buried in a common grave to the east of Sikanderbagh, marked by a tall cross which has since disappeared.

Standing on the roof of the Chattar Manzil Palace, Gubbins and his Residency companions could see the progress of their troops. From Sikanderbagh the men moved on to the Shah Najaf tomb, another high-walled building set in a garden. Sailors and soldiers with ropes dragged 24-pounder guns from the Naval Brigade into position, under heavy fire from the rebel batteries. The guns were positioned with their muzzles almost touching the exterior walls and began battering at them. A number of armed rebel Pasis on the walls fired arrows at troops of the 93rd Regiment, killing several, and were

'The Shah Nujeef', 1858. Felice Beato.

brought down with rifle fire at almost point-blank range. A cloud of smoke hung over the building and a rebel shell exploded in one of the British ammunition waggons, killing several men. Missiles of all kinds were thrown down on to the troops including brickbats and burning torches. Although the outer wall was partially breached, a high inner wall remained, but a quick-witted sergeant spotted that a breach had appeared in the north-east corner of the enclosure facing the river. Shots and shells had gone over the first breach and had blown out part of the wall on the far side. The tomb's defenders fled through the water gate and into the river, while British and Company troops got the front gates opened and gathered inside where they bivouacked for the night. A large quantity of gunpowder, both loose and in barrels, was found inside the central hall of the tomb together with 150 loaded shells. These were all removed the following day but rebel batteries in Badshahbagh, across the river, began firing at the tomb, believing the ammunition was still there and hoping that a lucky hit would blow it all up.

During the same long day, 16 November, other things were taking place. The battery installed in Phillips's garden, which it was intended to reveal suddenly by blowing down the garden wall, was not the success it was hoped. Because of the day's delay by Campbell in advancing into the city, the powder which had been laid around the wall had got damp during the cold night and did not fully ignite when primed. But two mines were successfully exploded under the Hiran Khana jail and by 3.30 p.m. that day a breach was made in the Qaisarbagh Palace and puffs of smoke seen from within the walls. Khurshid Manzil, headquarters of the military junta, seemed to have been abandoned, its bricked-up windows visible behind iron gratings. Now only the Moti Mahal Palace stood in the way of the evacuation from the Residency.

Photographs

There are no known photographs taken during the Uprising itself but a number of photographers arrived following the recapture, so there are images of the aftermath, including the avenue of felled trees in front of Dilkusha. Two of the most striking photographs were taken by Felice Beato, a young man born in Venice who was a British subject. Beato had applied for permission to visit India early in 1858 and arrived in Lucknow at the end of March. He recorded the hanging of two men from a gallows somewhere in the city. But his most disturbing photograph is of the interior of Sikanderbagh, showing gruesome skeletal remains and debris strewn across the courtyard in front of the garden pavilion. Here is the problem.

'Interior of Secundra Bagh, Lucknow, after the slaughter of two thousand rebels by the 93rd (Highlanders) Regiment of Foot', 1858. Felice Beato.

The battle for Sikanderbagh was fought on 16 November 1857. The Indian dead were dumped into trenches that had been dug outside the garden in a futile attempt to stop it from being captured. The British dead were buried a little further to the east under a small mound. According to a British medical officer, some Indian corpses were walled up within the garden house itself, piled into the east room, covered with earth and the door roughly plastered over. The courtyard and garden house were then cleansed so Campbell and his staff could move in straight away. This became the commander-in-chief's headquarters until the British evacuation of Lucknow less than a week later. It was also the place where Campbell welcomed the Residency refugees with tea and ginger biscuits on their journey to Dilkusha.

So Beato's photograph does not show the immediate aftermath of the battle for Sikanderbagh as the viewer might think, for there were no skeletons in the courtyard when he arrived in March 1858. A report on Beato at the scene stated that 'the great pile of bodies had been decently covered over' but that he insisted they be uncovered for the photograph 'before they were finally disposed of'. Almost certainly the bodies in Beato's photograph were those that had been walled up in the east room. In fact, the doorway is shown to the right of the picture with rubble and bricks in front of it, evidence of it having been recently unbricked and emptied before the whole pavilion was demolished.

'The Mess House [Khurshid Manzil] showing the fortifications,
Lucknow', 1858. Felice Beato.

On the following morning Campbell sent out detachments
under Brigadier Russell to secure four houses along the road to the
Martinière, including Banks's Bungalow, in order to guard his left
flank. Khurshid Manzil was bombarded by the Naval Brigade in case
any rebels were still lurking within it. When it was clear they had
fled, a regimental flag was hoisted from the roof. It was promptly shot
down from an adjoining roof of the Qaisarbagh Palace, still under
rebel control. It was put up again, and again shot down, this time
with a well-aimed shot through the flagstaff. It was propped up for the
third time and remained there, although firing continued. The wall of
Khurshid Manzil adjoined that of Moti Mahal, the last prize. Sappers
dug out openings in the wall through which troops entered, seeking
out the occupying rebels at the point of the bayonet and driving them
from room to room and finally out into the open, when a number
of them swam across the river into the shelter of Hazaribagh on the
opposite bank. A stretch of open ground was now all that separated
Campbell's forces from the garrison. Outram and Havelock rode
out with their staff officers to meet Campbell in front of Khurshid
Manzil, an iconic scene later captured in a fine painting by Thomas

Gateway to the Moti Mahal Palace, 1858. Felice Beato.

Barker. Havelock was grieved to learn that the casualties during the advance were about forty-three officers lost and 450 men killed or wounded. At the same time he was told he had been made a Knight Commander of the Bath, and was now Sir Henry.

'The Relief of Lucknow', after the painting by Thomas Barker, 1859. The three generals, Havelock, Outram and Campbell, meet in front of Khurshid Manzil.

Firing was still coming from the Qaisarbagh Palace east of the Residency and for the moment the last important site still in rebel hands. Again the Naval Brigade with heavy batteries stepped in and breached one of the main gateways, but went no further. Men who had survived the Residency siege claimed the whole palace could have been taken but this was not Campbell's intention. On the contrary, a rumour spread that Lucknow was to be completely abandoned within twenty-four hours. This did not come as a surprise to Outram because Campbell had already written to him on 10 November: 'I am here with a very weak force, deficient in all essentials. I have no ammunition for more than three days' firing; but I have come to hand out the wounded, women and children, and garrison, and I have not means to attempt anything more, and I shall be thankful to effect this. I shall blow up the Residency.' Luckily this last threat was not carried out.

Although forewarned, both Outram and Havelock were opposed to abandoning the city and this feeling was shared by those who had survived the siege and subsequent blockade of the Residency. 'We had defended the Residency post for nearly six months and now that our Force was strong in numbers, and stronger still in guns, we were to go, and to go in all the hurry and confusion attending a move on the brief notice of twenty-four hours,' wrote Gubbins indignantly. His indignation and that of others was compounded when Campbell refused to visit the battered garrison and remained in Sikanderbagh where he had made his temporary headquarters. (It was reported that Campbell was furious at being offered champagne by Gubbins while others were almost starving.) Feelings ran high on 18 November and the evacuation was postponed until the following day. This gave time for further preparations to be made. Transport of a sort was obtained, a few carriages, but mainly bullock carts, for the women and children. We have no details of the sums of money paid to their drivers but the evacuees were in no position to bargain. As many as 200 native guns of various calibres were in the Residency, some of which had been captured during the siege. These had to be destroyed in case they were suddenly seized and turned on the retreating force. Most had been spiked, that is, a metal spike had been hammered into the touch-hole. Now the spikes had to be tediously drilled out so the guns could be burst.

The women and children left in convoys at midday on 19 November, through the Baillie Guard gate, the Farhat Bakhsh and Chattar Manzil palaces, following the route by which Campbell had advanced four days earlier. The area of maximum danger was between the steam engine house and Moti Mahal, where they would be exposed to fire from the Qaisarbagh Palace. British sharpshooters were stationed on the parapets of Shah Najaf and Moti Mahal and a flying sap constructed, that is, a trench shielded on one side by tall baskets of stones. Even so, at this point, those who could were told to leave their carriages or carts and run along the trench keeping their heads down. The comparative safety of Sikanderbagh was reached

Chattar Manzil with the three-masted *Sultan of Oude* (centre) and the nawab's steam-powered fish boat (foreground), 1858. Felice Beato.

with little loss of life and here Campbell and his officers welcomed the refugees with ginger biscuits, bread and butter, and cups of tea with milk and sugar, all long-dreamed-of luxuries. The sandy country lanes between Sikanderbagh and Dilkusha were too difficult for the half-starved carriage horses, so doolies were provided for some and the rest had to walk. The procession started at 9 p.m. with some rebels hovering around and firing, but once into the country only the sound of jackals howling was heard until the safety of Dilkusha was reached around 2 a.m. on 20 November. Here, a small native bazaar had been established to supply the immediate wants of the refugees and here we leave them to make their way to Cawnpore, Allahabad, Calcutta and eventually home to England.

Dilkusha, east elevation, 1858. Captain J. Milliken.

The sick and wounded from the garrison were removed by the same route that evening and by dusk only fighting men were left in the garrison. The artillery followed them, together with the treasure and the last king's jewels, which were dug up from the lawn. Spare ammunition was thrown down the Residency wells which had provided potable water during the siege. In the evening of 22 November all remaining personnel left the site in silence and so quiet was the final evacuation that rebel troops near the Baillie Guard gate were unaware of their departure. General Havelock had been moved to Dilkusha, suffering from dysentery, and he died there on 24 November, comforted by his son, Lieutenant Harry Havelock. Such was the impact of his death that when news reached home and beyond, flags were flown at half-mast in New York. He rests today near Alambagh where a memorial was later erected over his tomb.

Although some officers and civilians believed that Lucknow should have been held, particularly after the sacrifices made and the buildings captured in the face of huge odds, Campbell was able to look at the broader picture of the British in northern India during this period, something which men deprived of any information for months had been unable to do. Delhi had been recaptured and the Company's capital, Calcutta was safe, despite sepoy mutinies in eastern Bengal. The Punjab was contained but in central India Company forces had faced thousands of determined rebels at Mandsaur, who were defeated on 23 November. Cawnpore was threatened once again by a force including the Gwalior Contingent led by Tantia Topi, attempting to reclaim the town for Nana Sahib.

Through the restored telegraph line between Alambagh and Cawnpore Campbell sought reassurance from Lord Canning, the governor general, that he was doing the correct thing by abandoning Lucknow. 'I have delayed further movement till I shall receive your Lordship's reply,' he telegraphed on 20 November. Canning replied the next day: 'The one step to be avoided is the total withdrawal of the British forces from Oudh. Your proposal to leave a strong moveable division with heavy artillery outside the city, and so to hold the city in check, will answer every purpose of policy.' On this assurance, Outram was left at Alambagh with around 4,000 men, too small a force to keep Lucknow in check, as the city made its own preparations for the assault that was surely to come.

The City in Winter: 23 November 1857 to 1 March 1858

When the rebel soldiers stationed near the Baillie Guard gate began their usual early morning round of shooting into the Residency on 23 November, they were surprised not to hear answering fire. According to a Lucknow resident, Kamal-ud-din Haider, who later wrote a journalistic account of the Uprising, it took several hours before they realized what had happened. The place they had so long coveted and fought for was suddenly theirs. A Pasi soldier sounded his trumpet, the men leapt roaring over the entrenchments and looting began. Whatever little was left after the garrison had gone was seized. Spent bullets, useless guns, wire and boxes of shells that had been thrown down the wells were hauled up. Gunny bags of small coin (pice) left in a shed were fought over while chairs, tables, beds, almirahs, glass, chinaware and iron pots were seized. 'Thousands of books', many of them no doubt the old Residency records, were sold cheaply to the local grocers who fashioned them into paper bags for their customers. A mine which had failed to detonate, suddenly exploded, killing fifteen men. Doors and window shutters were carried away for future use, and the recently buried dead were not left in peace as corpses were turned up in the search for treasure. From the safety of Alambagh, and through a telescope, British officers could see the new occupiers on the roof of the Residency. A curious proclamation was found pasted up in the Chattar Manzil. It stated that the British had not vacated the Residency and the palaces out of fear or in deference to the so-called king, but had left of their own accord, as a matter of expediency.

Whether this was indeed a parting shot or a hoax is unknown, although it has an authentic ring of defiance about it.

After the euphoria it was time to start preparing for the British return. An elite military council was formed, which included the powerful taluqdars Raja Jai Lal Singh of Azamgarh, Raja Beni Madho of Baiswara, the chief minister Sharaf-ud-daula, who had served under former nawabs, General Burkat Ahmed and Daroga Mammu Khan, in charge of the household and a trusted advisor to Begam Hazrat Mahal. The city was divided into four sectors. The Qaisarbagh Palace was at the centre, the citadel where the last stand would be made. To the south-east, the Haider canal became the first line of defence, a wet ditch, with a deep dry ditch dug between it and Banks's Bungalow. The Dilkusha and the Martinière, both of which had been easily captured and used as outposts by Campbell, were the far eastern sector, and across the river, Badshahbagh (a pleasure garden) and the Stone Bridge formed the northern sector. To the west, the

The Mermaid Gate, Qaisarbagh, 1858. Felice Beato.

old Daulat Khana just within the city's limits and Musabagh, three miles beyond, formed the last sector.

Within the sectors, plans were made for defence. Unlike Delhi, the city had never been walled, so huge embankments of earth were piled up, each with a dry ditch in front. Bastions of mud brick were constructed at intervals and loopholes through which a gun muzzle could be thrust. In addition, houses and enclosures were fortified and loopholed, and large gateways were bricked up. The Macchi Bhawan, though partially destroyed when its ammunition store was blown up, was still a viable defensive post. Traverses, deep ditches, were dug across the main streets which were also blockaded. Guns were placed at strategic points, including a strong battery at the end of Hazratganj where three roads meet, two of which led directly to Dilkusha and the Martinière. Hazratganj itself, today the main shopping centre, was strengthened specifically with an embankment starting from the river, passing in front of the Moti Mahal, encircling the Khurshid Manzil and joining the outer wall of the Sibtainabad

The Sibtainabad Imambara, Hazratganj, 1858. Felice Beato.

Imambara. Among the areas strengthened in anticipation of capture were Mohammedbagh (in today's cantonments), Aminabad, a popular bazaar, and the vital crossing point, the Stone Bridge. Each of these areas was allocated to different taluqdars with their own men, and reinforced by sepoys of the Oudh Force. Qaisarbagh had the largest number of people guarding it with 130 guns and wet ditches around it. The old Barood Khana, an earlier powder magazine and arsenal, was re-established and began casting guns for the coming conflict. An 18-pounder gun named Narak Munh (Hell-faced) was repaired and made ready for use. After the Gwalior Contingent and its many adherents had been finally defeated by Campbell and his brigadiers in Cawnpore on 6 December and pursued northwards to Bithur, a number of the defeated men made their way to Lucknow to join the rebel forces there.

Although from the outside and perhaps particularly from the British perspective too, Lucknow appeared a defensible city, there were serious divisions among its defenders. The fault line that ran between the royal household of Begam Hazrat Mahal with her son Birjis Qadr and the spiritual one of Maulvi Ahmadullah Shah, had deepened since the British left. The maulvi had been forced out of his headquarters, the Tarawali Kothi that stood adjacent to Khurshid Manzil, during the bombardment of the latter. He moved to Gaughat, west of the city, and began building a bridge of boats there across the river. Hazrat Mahal objected to this, quite possibly on the grounds of security, and sent Mammu Khan to stop the work. There was also the issue of different rates of pay for the sepoys. Those who had defected from the Oudh Irregular Force, mainly men who had been in the king's army before annexation, got Rs 12 per month, while the sepoys who had fled to Lucknow after the fall of Delhi in September got Rs 7 per month. Because the majority of the Delhi men supported the maulvi, this gave him the authority to challenge the begam. He accused her of maladministration but she suggested a

Daroga Mammu Khan, 1858. Digital image courtesy of the
Getty's Open Content Program.

conciliatory meeting. This was held on 18 December at Qaisarbagh,
with the maulvi's stipulation that neither the chief minister nor
Mammu Khan be present. The issue of disparate pay rates was ironed
out, every sepoy now receiving Rs 12 per month even though funds
were extremely low. It was agreed to keep the Oudh and the Delhi
forces separate to avoid disputes, which meant in effect that the two
forces were under two different leaders, the begam and the maulvi,
who were themselves in dispute.

The maulvi now agreed to send his Delhi troops eastward to halt
the rumoured advance of the Nepalese General Jang Bahadur and

his Gurkha Force. The Delhi men set out on 24 December towards Dariabad, but had not got very far when a horseman with a message halted them. Supposedly from the maulvi himself, the letter said that the object of the begam and the chief minister in sending them east was simply a device to get them out of Lucknow so the begam could hand the city over to the British. It was also suggested that harmony would not be restored until the chief minister was removed, if necessary, by force. It is possible that the letter, likely to be a forgery, was planted by the British, who were aware of the rift between the begam and the maulvi. Disinformation, used judiciously, was a useful tool, employed by both sides. The Delhi men immediately turned round and headed back to Lucknow. Tension was high and two weeks later fighting broke out between the Delhi sepoys and the Oudh sepoys near the north-west gateway of Qaisarbagh. A hundred men from both sides were killed and fighting only ceased when the begam herself came out of the palace and intervened, supported by Captain Suba Singh who shouted 'Raj Mata ki jai!' (Long live the Queen Mother!) which brought the men to their senses.

Alambagh, through which the evacuees from the Residency had passed the previous November, continued to be held by Outram, as Canning had directed. It acted as both an irritant, visible from the city and as a reminder that the British had not gone away. Today the ruined building stands separated from its gatehouse and the large garden that surrounded it by buildings and shacks, making it difficult to appreciate just how strongly it was defended. The palace itself is small, a two-storeyed compact building, so having placed piquets there, Outram encamped his main force a mile away on an open plain straddling the Cawnpore Road. The tented encampment extended from a village to the west as far east as Jallalabad fort, and the whole area occupied a circuit of about eleven miles. During the early days it had been difficult to find supplies for horses and men.

Soldiers on the roof of Alambagh, 1858. Patrick Fitzgerald.

Part of Outram's camp at Alambagh, 1858. Lance Corporal E.W. Jones,
National Army Museum.

Villages around the area refused to provide grass and grains, either because they had little surplus or because they had been warned not to, by the military junta. Foraging parties had to travel further and further afield and the plight of the villagers, faced with armed Company soldiers but fearful of the wrath of the junta, was pitiable. To be accused of spying for the British was a handy weapon to fling at an enemy or a rival but to be found collaborating with the British could lead to death. Nevertheless, Kamal-ud-din Haider reports that not only did the soldiers pay for what they took, they also bought goods from enterprising local traders, supplying what the villagers could not, or dare not. Goods were smuggled in secretly at night, including liquor from Cawnpore and grain at extortionate prices.

The position had eased after Cawnpore was recaptured by the British early in December and the road reopened. Outram sent fortnightly convoys back and forth, guarded each time by 450 men, bringing in much-needed supplies and reinforcements. But the convoys themselves, scanning the roadsides for rebels as they rode along, were an added source of danger for the Alambagh garrison. Every convoy automatically reduced the number of men Outram had at his disposal, which were few enough anyway, as he pointed out. Holding the garrison as well as Jallalabad fort absorbed about 600 men and after deducting the sick and wounded this left little more than 2,000 men to fend off rebel attacks. Spies kept the opposition informed when the convoys left and attacks were timed in the hope that fewer men in the garrison might increase the chance of wiping it out altogether. Nine separate attacks were made during the twelve weeks that Outram held Alambagh. All were unsuccessful, resulting in great loss of rebel lives.

G.W. Forrest, who later wrote the *History of the Indian Mutiny* drawing on officers' reports and government papers, commented that 'the sepoys proved by their heavy losses that it was not courage

Jallalabad fort. Lieutenant-Colonel D.S. Dodgson, *General Views and Special Points of Interest of the City of Lucknow,* 1860.

in which they were lacking, but, as at Delhi, leadership. If they had been led by men acquainted with the operations of war, the English commander [Outram] would have found it impossible to hold his extended position and keep open his communication with Cawnpore.' He could have added that the garrison had the advantage of far superior weaponry than the opposition. During several attacks, rebel sepoys advancing bravely towards Alambagh were mown down at close range by Enfields and heavy guns while others found their retreat cut off because a British detachment had ridden around to their rear and was able to herd them back to the city. Many simply fled in the face of unrelenting fire, pushing their guns into ravines, from where they were retrieved by the British. As many as 30,000 rebels were estimated to have attacked the garrison on 12 January 1858, dividing themselves into two groups to tackle simultaneously the right and left flanks of the defenders. As they drew nearer they were met by the concentrated artillery and musket fire of the 74th Regiment which drove them back. After two further attacks, and two further repulses on the same day, an attempt was made to attack the central position of the troops, but this too failed. The greater the number of attackers, the greater the death toll. Four days later another prolonged rebel attack was led by a Hindu devotee, Barkhe Das, dressed as Hanuman, the monkey god. Barkhe Das had been a risaldar, a native cavalry officer in the king's army, and was posted with the opposition at Alambagh. According to local reports he got as far as Outram's tent, in an unsuccessful bid to assassinate him, shouting 'Remember Sikanderbagh' in an odd echo of British soldiers shouting 'Remember Cawnpore' as they rampaged through Awadh. Barkhe Das was shot down with his followers.

Maulvi Ahmadullah Shah was carried to Alambagh in a palanquin to witness an opposition attack on 15 February and ten days later, during the final attempt, Begam Hazrat Mahal, her son Birjis Qadr, the chief minister and other nobles rode out on elephants to encourage their men. By now more British reinforcements had arrived including Hodson's Horse, the 7th Hussars and the 1st Bengal Fusiliers. There were heavy rebel casualties and the royal party turned and fled. The begam was reported to have criticized her own Oudh Force for failing to capture Alambagh but in truth it had proved impossible in spite of very superior numbers.

Seizing the moment, the governor general Lord Canning instructed Outram to offer a peace treaty to the begam on behalf of the East India Company. A lakh of rupees per annum (equivalent then to £10,000) was offered as a pension and her security was guaranteed. Outram's letter was tossed scornfully aside. At the end of January 1858 the begam was told by the elderly rebel leader Kanwar Singh that the British had reached an agreement with the Nepalese leader Jang Bahadur. His Gurkha troops would assist in the recapture of Lucknow in return for the town of Gorakhpur, near Awadh's north-eastern border, and a substantial share of the anticipated loot and prize money when the city fell. Hazrat Mahal sent a counter-offer to Jang Bahadur, promising him not only Gorakhpur, but the towns of Azamgarh, Arrah and Benares as well. She sent two men, disguised as faqirs, to make the offer, but they were both captured by the British and put to death. So the final disposition of native troops was made and six generals selected, including Raja Jai Lal Singh, who had coordinated Lucknow's defences, the stalwart Raja of Mahmudabad and the maulvi. The begam did not lead the army, contrary to popular belief, but remained in the Qaisarbagh Palace, relying on her generals.[3]

The British decision to recapture the city early in 1858 was by no means unanimous. The commander-in-chief, Campbell, had told governor general Canning that it would be impossible to subdue, much less to hold the province, with less than 30,000 men. Canning felt that 'so long as Oudh is not dealt with, there will be no real quiet on this side of India. Every sepoy who has not already mutinied or deserted will have a standing temptation to do so, and every native chief will grow to think less and less of our power.' By

Sir Colin Campbell. Photographer unknown.

the end of December 1857, Canning had somewhat modified his
view and thought it was not necessary to subdue the whole province
at once. '... [I]f it were possible to collect a force equal to taking
Lucknow and holding it without attempting more for the present,
it should be done.' Lucknow had become a symbol of survival since
the rescue of the besieged Britons from the Residency. Even though
the city could not be held then, it stood as a counterpoint to the
massacres of Britons at Cawnpore. Canning was quicker to realize
this than Campbell who wanted to delay the recapture until the
autumn of 1858 in order to deal with Rohilkhand first, an area to the
north-west of Awadh. The governor general pointed out that places
as far apart as Ava in Burma and Hyderabad in southern India were
keenly interested in the fate of Lucknow. Subtle pressure was added
when Outram added that if the recapture was delayed then he would
recommend 'as Chief Commissioner of Oudh' withdrawing his forces
nearer to Cawnpore as it was not possible to exercise civil government
if not in possession of the capital itself. He added, from direct
experience, that 'remaining in the vicinity of the city without making
any effort to take it, would be a declaration of weakness which, under
the present circumstances, is in every way to be deprecated'. If the
recapture was planned for the spring, then Alambagh must be held.
There was clearly tension between Campbell and Outram, which is
why the latter said he was speaking not as a military man (although
he was clearly a fine soldier) but as the chief commissioner. Campbell
had to agree to an early recapture. Worries about too few men to
make this viable had been eased with the Nepalese leader's offer of
help, which was accepted, and around 8,000 Gurkha troops began
a slow advance towards Lucknow.

The recapture: 4 to 19 March 1858

Preparations began as soon as Campbell had acquiesced in the Spring offensive but were kept secret as long as possible. Two 68-pounders were sent upriver from Allahabad to Cawnpore for their onward journey to Lucknow. These enormous iron cannon, first cast in England in 1841, measured ten feet in length and had a range of 1.5–2 miles. The siege train was sent up from Agra, a convoy of men, ammunition and vehicles that extended for some twelve miles and was not scheduled to reach Cawnpore until the first week of February. Campbell had stationed himself at Fatehgarh, the cantonment above Cawnpore, in a decoy move and pretence that he intended to attack Rohilkhand. Jang Bahadur was not expected to arrive until the end of February. Lord Canning, who had temporarily moved his office from Calcutta to Allahabad to be nearer the final assault, told Campbell that he had to wait for the Nepalese ruler: 'It would drive him wild to find himself jockeyed out of all share in the great campaign ...' and of course the great opportunity for loot. Unaware of the reasons for the delayed move on Lucknow, there was criticism from some quarters of Campbell for letting the cold weather season slip away. By the beginning of March, the temperature was rising and men could find themselves fighting in 80 degrees Fahrenheit.

Sir Thomas Harte Franks who had fought in the First Anglo-Sikh War, was on his way home on sick leave when the Uprising broke out, so he remained in Calcutta until he was well enough to take up active service again. An Irishman who was described as having a 'fiery violent nature, and a martinet of the old school', he was appointed in January 1858 to command the Jaunpore Force, with the rank of brigadier-general. After winning a decisive battle against a rebel force led by the nazim, Mehndi Hussain, near Sultanpur, Franks marched north-west and by 9 March was at headquarters Camp,

Dilkusha. He had cleared the way for Jang Bahadur's troops, whose slow progress, estimated at only six miles a day, was hampered by the soldiers' wives and other camp followers.

Meanwhile, Campbell and his advance force had moved across country from the Alambagh camp towards Dilkusha at the beginning of March. The heavy guns, mounted on waggons and each drawn along the road by six horses, were accompanied by infantry and cavalry on either side, with the baggage train in the rear. Relatively easy to transport along the metalled Cawnpore Road, the circuitous route from Alambagh to the Dilkusha through sandy soil and hostile villages was much harder and it was not until 4 March that everything was in place. Now Campbell was in command of all the open ground on the south-eastern margin of Lucknow, batteries and regiments spread out in a long line between the Dilkusha park and the Mohammedbagh garden and at a right angle to the Gomti river. The sappers, part of Brigadier Napier's Engineers Force, established themselves in Bibiapur House, an elegant Palladian-style villa that had once served as overnight accommodation for important guests on their way to and from the city.

Bibiapur Kothi today. Tulika Sahu.

It was Robert Napier who had suggested the plan of attack to
Campbell while the two men were waiting at Fatehgarh. It was not
dissimilar to the second, successful relief in November the previous
year, avoiding the pinch-point of the Charbagh bridge, crossing the
canal and swinging widely to the east of the city before dropping
down to Sikanderbagh. This time the circuit to the east was to be even
wider, going as far as Ismaelganj on the Faizabad Road, the scene of
the Chinhat disaster the previous June. The Recapture Force was to
be divided into two unequal parts. Outram and his First Division,
moving quickly, were to attack the city from the north bank of the
Gomti, from the one area that had not been considered vulnerable
or even feasible by the military junta, for they had made virtually no
defensive preparations here. The Second, Third and Fourth Divisions
were to push up from the Dilkusha base, capturing a number of
strategic buildings as they fought their way towards the Qaisarbagh
citadel, the seat of the rebel government headed by the begam and
her son. If this could be taken, then the battle was won. Both sides
knew this.

The Haider canal had been deepened during the winter as the
first line of defence, with a steep embankment on the city side. But
the Gomti was fordable, with the water level dropping considerably
before the monsoon season. Two floating bridges were constructed
to cross the river before it met the canal. They were ingeniously
fashioned from empty beer casks, of which the British regiments
no doubt had a plentiful supply. The barrels were lashed by ropes
to timber cross-pieces and floated into position, before a sturdy
roadway of planking was laid on top. It had to be strong enough
to bear the weight of the heaviest guns, the ammunition waggons,
horses and men. Working parties spent 4 and 5 March building the
bridges and the jetties that joined them to the riverbanks. Outram,
now finally released from Alambagh, which was left in the care of

The Haider canal today. Anil Mehrotra.

Brigadier Franklin, marched the First Division over the bridges in the early morning mist of 6 March, pitching his camp at Ismaelganj, eight miles east of Lucknow. The following day the lower bridge was dismantled, moved downstream and re-erected near Bibiapur

House so the siege train could cross it and join Outram. The initial stages of the recapture were more to do with engineering than fighting, although there were constant attacks on the men building the batteries, digging entrenchments, erecting and dismantling the bridges, and laying temporary walkways.

Campbell's plan was to avoid the street fighting that had cost over a thousand lives during the first relief as soldiers struggled to get to the Residency. He was going to enter Qaisarbagh through a carefully worked out route that involved taking a small number of strategic buildings, one after the other, and employing heavy artillery from each newly captured building to reach the next, all of this under intense fire from the defenders. It is difficult today to imagine this part of Lucknow as it was in 1858. Of the buildings targeted by Campbell, the Martinière, Banks's Bungalow, the Begam Kothi, the Sibtainabad Imambara, the Chini Bazaar and finally Qaisarbagh, only the first two retain their spacious grounds. In fact, Banks's Bungalow, which later became Government House and is today Raj Bhawan, was built in the grounds of the Martinière, before the Haider canal cut across the land. Of the remaining buildings that Campbell had to capture, the Begam Kothi was demolished in the 1980s; the Sibtainabad Imambara, although retaining its central courtyard, had its gatehouse area compromised by the Maqbara Road running across it and intrusive shops, the Chini Bazaar retains only an isolated gatehouse and Qaisarbagh was later deliberately reduced so that only its central garden remains today, bordered by terraces of houses.

As Campbell's assaults began on 9 March, Outram's men moved along the Faizabad Road towards Lucknow and the isolated buildings and gardens on the north bank of the river. Elephants drew the heavy guns along the sandy path through dense jungle until they reached the king's racecourse and its grandstand, the Chakkarwali Kothi, a circular building. Thought by Outram to have been abandoned, it was in fact now occupied by the maulvi and a number of his followers after another dispute with the chief minister, Sharaf-ud-daula, whom the maulvi had unjustly accused of being in league with the British. It was to the advantage of the British, says Kamal-ud-din Haider, that these daily quarrels were going on between rival factions of the opposition. After a deputation from Mammu Khan, speaking for the Qaisarbagh-based government, most of the maulvi's men returned to the city, leaving him with too few soldiers to defend the grandstand. Those who remained did what they could from the ground floor rooms, killing three British officers and nine men, before the building was shelled, and its occupants killed or fled with their wounded. The colours, the flag of the Bengal Fusiliers, was hoisted from the top of the kothi as a signal of success to Campbell at the

'The Chukkur Kothee on the Left bank of the Goomtee', Lieutenant-Colonel D.S. Dodgson, *General Views and Special Points of Interest of the City of Lucknow*, 1860.

Dilkusha headquarters. The distance between the two buildings was about three miles, but the ground there was flat, criss-crossed by the winding Gomti, two low-roofed villages and the *talab* or lake in front of the Martinière. Outram's force continued to march west along the riverbank until it reached Badshahbagh, a royal game park with a pavilion overlooking a small artificial canal. Again, it was stoutly walled and its gates had to be blown open with gunpowder charges. An estimated 800 rebels were killed during its capture. The garden was an important strategic site because it stood directly opposite the Qaisarbagh Palace across the river. It was from Badshahbagh, where the eight 24-pounder guns and the three 8-inch howitzers were entrenched, that the city's palaces were battered.

African Soldiers

Accounts of the Uprising mention a number of African men and women fighting with the rebels against the British. One such sharpshooter was nicknamed 'Bob the Nailer' because his accurate fire 'nailed' or killed people in the Residency garrison. Bob was shooting from an upper window of Johannes's House, overlooking the vulnerable south-east perimeter. Another African soldier with a rifle and telescope stationed himself at the top of the Clock Tower that stood directly in front of the Baillie Guard gate. A third man was spotted defending the Martinière, firing from a window, gorgeously attired in a yellow silk robe according to one account. Bodies of African soldiers were found after the first relief in the river palace courtyards.

The most celebrated African soldier was a woman, one of the 2,000 people defending Sikanderbagh on 16 November 1857. Company and British soldiers in the garden were being shot down by someone up a tall tree. Rifle fire was directed into the branches and eventually a body came crashing down on to the flagstones. When her pink silk blouse burst open, she was found to be an African woman, who had clearly been a deadly shot with one of the new Enfield rifles.

The last king, Wajid Ali Shah, had recruited a number of Africans for his Hubshiyan Risala or Black Cavalry unit, formed from men brought to India by Arab slave traders. He also had a number of female African soldiers as his bodyguard, who were probably part of the Gulabi (Rose) Pultan. African men guarded the royal treasury in Qaisarbagh, and African women not only guarded the royal zenana, but some were inside it too as wives of the king.

The African soldiers, men and women who survived the Uprising and remained in Lucknow after its recapture said their loyalty was to the king, their master. As a group they were poorly treated by the British government and today only a few families of African descent remain in the city.

Around 2 p.m., after Campbell had seen the Fusiliers' flag flying from the racecourse grandstand, he ordered an assault to begin on the Martinière School, which had already been captured twice during the previous reliefs and now needed to be taken again for the third and final time. The guns of three batteries were trained on the building, and began pounding away. A peculiarity of the Martinière was that it had not been built entirely of small lakhori brick, but also incorporated larger *pan-patta* bricks, which were harder to penetrate. Shot and shell were poured into the occupied building for three to four hours and rocket tubes from Peel's Naval Brigade were fired into the trenches in the gardens. Finally great holes appeared in the outer walls, and the parapets with their elaborate balustrades and stucco statues were brought down. It is a testament to its architect Claude Martin that in spite of extensive shelling and the loss of much external decoration, the building, then sixty years old, remained structurally intact, as it does today. The opposition fell back after musket fire was directed into the gardens, but not before Peel had been wounded in the thigh. Once the building was secured, Campbell rode over to it and climbed up its single winding staircase to the top from where he could see Outram's men at work across the river.

The Martinière today.

Outram intended to enfilade the first line of defence, the wet ditch and its embankment that ran along the city side of the canal. Three guns and a howitzer were brought into play. But the lines were empty, the opposition had fled. Lieutenant Thomas Butler of the 1st Bengal European Fusiliers swam dramatically across the river to inform Campbell at the Martinière and to advise him to get men to occupy the deserted rebel batteries. This was done and the Highland Regiment moved in. Butler then swam dramatically back across the river and was subsequently awarded the coveted VC.

After the Martinière was secured, Banks's Bungalow was the next target, but there were not enough heavy guns in place that day to capture it, so Campbell postponed the assault. The following day,

Banks's Bungalow, 1858. Felice Beato.

10 March, artillery was brought up and a battery of four guns, one howitzer and three 8-inch mortars established in the far corner of the Martinière park, facing the bungalow. Campbell planned to turn the ungainly two-storey building with its thatched roofs into a strong military post and it was here that Battery No. 4-1 was constructed with four guns and eight mortars, to bombard the Begam Kothi and its complex of buildings that formed the southern point of the second line of defence. More guns were placed to the right of the bungalow to fire at the batteries constructed at the junction of Hazratganj and the roads to Dilkusha and the Martinière. At the same time, Outram on the north bank had sent troops out to secure the Dilaram, a two-storey English-style house that stood directly across the river opposite the Chattar Manzil Palace on the south bank from where heavy firing had begun. Rebel fighters within the building were chased to a neighbouring village which was then set alight by Outram's men, who reportedly also seized and killed a number of harmless dhobis (washermen and women) cleansing clothes in the river. A large crowd of townspeople had gathered as spectators around the Shish Mahal, one of the palaces in the old Daulat Khana complex. They were observing a British officer, telescope to his eye, surveying the

south bank. An unnamed rebel cavalry officer crossed the river, shot the officer dead and rode back to shouts of 'Shabash!' (Bravo!). The cavalryman was particularly commended for not removing the head of the deceased officer. A number of decapitated British heads on poles had been put up on the Akbari Darwaza, the gate at the lower end of the Chowk, the main street in the old city. The going rate, according to Kamal-ud-din Haider, was Rs 100 for an officer's head and Rs 50 for a soldier's.

The Begam Kothi, Campbell's next target, on the southern side of Hazratganj, had been built in 1844, so it was not a particularly old building, nor was it fortified like the Macchi Bhawan. The kothi's high walls, both the outer and the inner walls, were there to protect the begams, the royal ladies, from the vulgar gaze of passers-by. The test of a modest building housing noble ladies was that a man standing on the back of an elephant should not be able to look over its walls. The kothi turned out to be particularly difficult to penetrate. Firing went on continuously during the night of 11 March. Mortars sent up flights of shells which were poetically described as falling stars on the city. Peel's heavy guns were brought up and battered away. Clouds of brick dust rose from the building and through it rebel sepoys could be seen swarming on the roofs of the adjacent buildings. It seemed impossible to make a breach in the outer wall, until 4.30 in the afternoon, when listeners heard the cannonading cease to be replaced with the sound of musketry, which meant that the storming brigade under Adrian Hope had got in at last. The 93rd Highlanders, 4th Punjab Rifles and Gurkha troops divided into two flanks, the right reaching the high outer wall of the kothi where they found a huge parapet of earth with a steep scarp and a ditch nearly eighteen feet wide and ten feet deep. A striking photograph taken two weeks later by the photographer Felice Beato illustrated the obstacles that the men had to overcome.

'The Battery near the Begum Kotee, Lucknow, 1858'. Note that
the photograph has been doctored. The eastern corner of the palace
disappears abruptly and a ruined wall has been inserted, 1858.
Felice Beato.

Climbing across and through a breach finally punched in the wall
by Peel's guns, the troops found it undefended. A second high wall
inside was climbed to reveal a number of windows crudely bricked
up. The bricks were pickaxed out and soldiers shoved themselves
through into the dark narrow passages that led to the inner courtyard
of the building. Interior doorways and gates had been barricaded
and rebel sepoys, more familiar with the building, were at the end of
every corridor and corner. They were driven back at bayonet point
by the Highlanders and Sikhs during a fierce battle that lasted two
hours. The left flank drove the rebels through the intricate building
and outbuildings towards the Sibtainabad Imambara further along
Hazratganj and as far as the final line of defence around Qaisarbagh.
In order to winkle out rebels hiding in the small dark rooms of the

Interior of the now demolished Begam Kothi, Hazratganj, 1976.
Author's collection.

ground floor bags of gunpowder were lit with a short fuse and hurled
in. As night fell, hundreds of rebel corpses, some still smouldering
in their cotton clothes, were piled up in the courtyards. Campbell
described the battle of the Begam Kothi as 'the sternest struggle
which occurred during the siege'. During the fighting Brigadier
William Hodson, who had ridden over to the kothi and dismounted
to enter it, was fatally shot in one of the lower rooms. Some reports
claimed he had been caught in the act of looting, while others took
care to exonerate him. Hazrat Mahal was said to have offered a
substantial reward to the person who killed him, and he may have
been deliberately targeted. Hodson was carried to Banks's Bungalow
where he died the following day and was buried in the grounds of
the Martinière.

Major William Hodson's tomb today at La Martinière. Courtesy of
Carlyle McFarland.

On the same day the Begam Kothi was taken, the Nepalese leader
Jang Bahadur arrived with his Gurkha troops and was formally
received by Campbell at the Dilkusha headquarters. A guard of
honour provided by the 42nd Highlanders with their drums and
bagpipes was laid on, a large *shamiana* or canopy erected and
Campbell changed out of his work clothes into his general's uniform
of scarlet, gold lace and cocked hat. Jang Bahadur had been expected
at 4 p.m. and the commander-in-chief was ready. Time slipped by.
Campbell paced up and down waiting, one hand behind his back.
Noise from the assault on the Begam Kothi could clearly be heard
at the Dilkusha. Finally, at 4.30 p.m. a startling figure appeared, his

red jacket covered in jewels, wearing white kid gloves and a plume of bird-of-paradise feathers 'delicately beaded with emeralds and diamonds' on his head. Taking off his sunglasses which he habitually wore, Jang Bahadur shook hands with Campbell and the two generals sat exchanging compliments before the Highland band marched past 'playing a heart-stirring pibroch'. The Nepalese leader with twenty-five field guns, drawn into position by his men, in lieu of horses, was requested to relieve the Company's men at the newly captured Begam Kothi.

Jang Bahadur, ruler of Nepal. Photographer unknown.

On 12 March, two of Napier's British engineers and four Indian assistants climbed Qadam-i-Rasool, the small artificial hill overlooking Shah Najaf on the south bank of the river. From here the men were able to look down on to the tomb in its walled enclosure and found that it had been abandoned. 'A sharp musketry fire was opened' from an adjoining site but with reinforcements of two hundred men and fifty sappers, the tomb was made defensible. Sikanderbagh, the scene of intense fighting the previous November, had already been retaken without opposition.

Across the river Outram set up a battery in front of Badshahbagh and opened fire on Qaisarbagh, an extensive set of buildings and gardens completed only four years earlier and said to rival Versailles in size. What remains today is only the central garden courtyard of a much larger complex, together with an adjoining enclosure containing two tombs of an earlier nawab and one of his wives. At the same time, Outram was advancing towards the Iron Bridge that crossed the river just west of the Residency garrison and which was defended by the Jafri Pultan. His men were able to capture the northern end of the bridge, but with the loss of Lieutenant William Moorsom, who had been guiding the column and had an intimate knowledge of the city. Attempting to seize the northern end of the Stone Bridge as well, Outram's men met heavy resistance and had to withdraw.

Looking towards the White Barahdari in Qaisarbagh, c. 1867.
John Edward Saché.

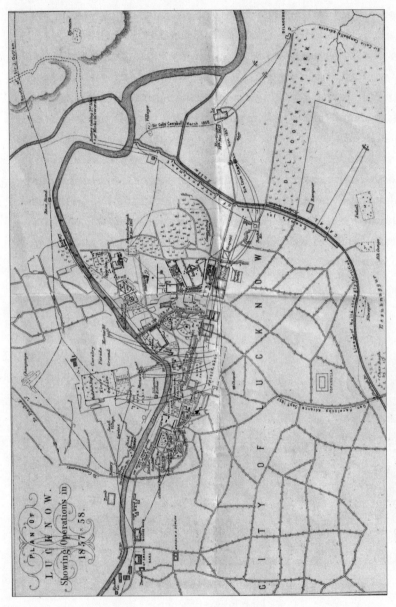

'Plan of Lucknow Showing Operations in 1857-58'. William Mackenzie, London, Edinburgh and Glasgow.

On the south bank, Napier and his engineers were punching
their way along Hazratganj through the buildings on the south side
of the street, avoiding the actual road. With the Begam Kothi now
secure, the next target was the Sibtainabad Imambara. Reaching
what is today Halwasiya Marg, the engineers continued to work their

Sibtainabad Imambara today. Anil Mehrotra.

way forward under fierce musketry fire, while heavy guns pounded
the Imambara, including round shot from the naval brigade guns
across the river. By the morning of 14 March two breaches had been
made in the wall. A storming party of two companies of HM 10th
Foot and Brasyer's Sikhs waited, while sappers with scaling ladders,
bags of gunpowder and tools stood ready. Rebel sepoys lining the

walls and roofs of adjoining houses continued with musket fire but 68-pounder cannonballs from Outram's gunners effectively ended this particular fight and Major Brasyer himself with his Sikh soldiers was seen clearing the houses and blowing open the outer wall. The storming party entered through the second breach and as soon as the Imambara was secured, it pressed on to the Nur Bakhsh Kothi, another palatial house standing in its own grounds. From its roof the men could look down into the eastern end of Qaisarbagh, its third line of defence running in front of the walls.

Brigadier Russell, commanding the 5th Brigade, now urged caution but according to subsequent official government reports, 'The Sikhs could not be restrained.' Having pursued the rebel sepoys through the Imambara court and the Nur Bakhsh Kothi enclosures, they found themselves in one of the outlying courtyards of Qaisarbagh. Support came again from Sikh soldiers led by Brasyer, and men of the 90th whom Lieutenant Harry Havelock had brought up. They climbed on to the flat roofs of the Qaisarbagh buildings and began firing down into the last entrenchment and its bastions. Men from HM 10th Foot arrived and although initially the rebel soldiers seemed to have the advantage, firing from the loopholed buildings in the palace grounds, Havelock and a party of Sikhs charged along the entrenchment outside the Chini Bazaar gateway, seized two further bastions and drove the opposing sepoys further into the palace.

At his Dilkusha headquarters, Campbell was informed that his men were in the palace. He rode to the Imambara, and climbing its steps consulted with Napier and Franks. The commander-in-chief had expected the fiercest resistance to come from troops defending Qaisarbagh and had planned his assault for the following day, 15 March. But now it could be taken. A hundred and fifty of Brasyer's Sikhs and fifty men of the 97th Foot breached the Chini Bazaar and entered the enclosure with its two large tombs. This led directly to the central garden courtyard of the palace with its numerous follies and marble pavilions. The intrusion of the soldiers was met with further fire from the palace windows which initially drove them to seek shelter at one of the two great gateways, which still survive. The final picture is confused, but a gun belonging to the palace defenders was captured, further British and Company troops arrived and the rebels were driven across the courtyard. Begam Hazrat Mahal and her advisors seem to have remained in Qaisarbagh until almost the last moment. Persuaded to escape, her small party went first to the chief minister's house where they sheltered for a few hours before moving on to the Daulat Khana on their way to Musabagh.

Firing continued from the palace windows but room after room was taken and it was now that the infamous looting of Qaisarbagh began when the journalist William Russell reported in a memorable phrase that he saw men 'drunk with plunder' stagger out with priceless jewellery and treasure. Looting continued until nightfall and started again the following day, 15 March, until Campbell ordered it to stop. The more goods that were stolen, the less prize money

The Iron Bridge, 1858. Felice Beato.

was available for the officers and men. The rapid fall of Qaisarbagh had taken the British by surprise and it had a demoralizing effect on its defenders. Company and British forces holding Sikanderbagh and other posts at the second line of defence were ordered to move forward and buildings captured during the second relief in November were recaptured again, including Moti Mahal, Khurshid Manzil, Tarawali Kothi and Chattar Manzil, the river palace.

Across the river fierce fighting had continued on 14 March around the Iron Bridge between the opposition and Outram's men. The bridge had been barricaded with sandbags and these were removed under heavy fire by an officer and sergeant of the Royal Engineers. Outram had expected to receive an order, via field telegraph, from Campbell to cross the bridge and continue to move westward along the south bank where other major sites including the Macchi Bhawan and the Great Imambara were still in opposition hands. Inexplicably to many observers, including Lieutenant Roberts, Campbell forbade Outram to cross the bridge if there was the chance of 'losing a single man'. With a 9-pounder rebel gun sweeping the bridge this could not be guaranteed, so Outram and the 5th Brigade remained on the north bank only to see a flood of refugees and large bodies of armed rebels fanning out from the city across both bridges and fleeing east along the Faizabad Road and west to Musabagh. Half-hearted attempts were made by the cavalry to intercept them and Campbell himself rode out towards Sandeela, some thirty miles north-west of Lucknow. But it was too late. 'Not a judicious move on Sir Colin's part to send the cavalry miles away from Lucknow just when they could have been usefully employed on the outskirts of the city,' commented Roberts. The cavalry brigades returned empty-handed two days later, although as some observers noted, it saved Campbell the problem of what to do with hundreds of defeated but armed men.

The Stone Bridge, 1858. Felice Beato

On 16 March, leaving Brigadier Walpole and the 3rd Division to guard both the Iron and the Stone Bridges, Outram was ordered to the south bank, but had to march his men eastwards down to the bridge of casks opposite Sikanderbagh then march them westwards up to Qaisarbagh. Here a track had been laid towards the Residency, and although there was token firing, the 23rd Fusiliers rushed through the Baillie Guard gate and entered the site so dearly held the previous year. A further two companies of the 23rd, accompanied by Captain Gould Weston, a former ADC who had lived in Lucknow for several years, advanced westwards, capturing the 9-pounder brass gun at the Iron Bridge. From the Residency the Madras Artillery, formerly under the Brigadier Neill, kept up heavy firing on Macchi Bhawan using the two 68-pounder guns of the Naval Brigade and mortars.

As the troops guided by Captain Weston were led through a labyrinth of lanes and streets to the Macchi Bhawan, its former defenders fled and were chased into the outer courtyard of the

Loot

An extraordinary amount of loot was taken from the Lucknow palaces by British, Sikh and Gurkha soldiers during the recapture of March 1858. A figure of twelve million sterlings' worth has been suggested. This cannot be verified but Sergeant William Forbes-Mitchell, who served with the 93rd Highlanders, says enough caskets of treasure were smuggled home in the uniform cases of officers to pay off mortgaged estates, including 'one deeply encumbered estate which was cleared of mortgage to the tune of £180,000 within two years of the plunder of Lucknow'.

The largest item taken was a complete marble kiosk from Qaisarbagh, carefully dismantled, shipped to England and presented to Queen Victoria to commemorate the end of the Uprising. It was re-erected in the gardens of Frogmore House, part of the royal palace of Windsor, where it is known today as the Indian kiosk. Queen Victoria also got a splendidly illustrated manuscript called the *Ishqnama,* the autobiography of the last king of Awadh, Wajid Ali Shah. This was presented to her by Sir John Lawrence, who in turn had got it from Sikh soldiers looting Qaisarbagh.[4]

The Qaisarbagh kiosk at Frogmore Estate, Windsor, presented to Queen Victoria by Lord Canning to mark the end of the 'Indian Mutiny'.

Captain Gould Weston took two valuable Qurans from the Great Imambara during its capture and he also raided the house of the court photographer, Ahmad Ali Khan, carrying away a number of pictures of the royal household plus two wooden boxes of glass negatives of the city and its inhabitants before 1857.[5]

Colin Campbell was presented with two rather florid paintings taken from a reception room in Qaisarbagh. Full of naked cherubs and heroic classical figures, Campbell quickly passed them on to the Royal Engineers Mess at Chatham, where they remain today.

Great Imambara. The Fusiliers rushed up the stairs of the handsome building and into its large central hall decorated with mirrors, chandeliers and a pair of green glass tigers. The Imambara was occupied and five 8-inch mortars put in position while the 79th Highlanders captured the adjoining Rumi Darwaza and the Jama Masjid. Here a large quantity of gunpowder collected by the opposition was discovered and Outram ordered it to be thrown down a deep well so it could not be retrieved. As the bags went down, one struck the side of the well and the resulting explosion set off the powder carts, killing two officers and forty men, more than had been killed in capturing the Imambara site. The officers were buried in one of Qaisarbagh's gardens.

The Rumi Darwaza, 1858. Felice Beato.

By 17 March the recapture of Lucknow was almost completed although firing was still heard from the city. An opportunistic attack by the rebels on Alambagh, with its reduced number of defenders, was beaten off. Jang Bahadur's Gurkhas occupied Charbagh and secured the Cawnpore Road. An unsuccessful attack by the opposition led to the capture of ten of their guns and the waggons of a field battery. Outram continued to push westwards, capturing and holding the Daulat Khana, the Hussainabad Imambara and the house of the chief minister, where the begam had halted on her way to Musabagh.

Musabagh, 1976. Author's collection.

Meanwhile the maulvi had escaped into the city, to an old religious shrine, Dargah Hazrat Abbas. Here he holed up with a large number of his supporters, the Delhi Force soldiers, who put up a fierce resistance when attacked in the shrine by Brigadier Lugard, the 93rd Highlanders and the 4th Punjab Rifles on 21 March. Also here, surprisingly, was Sharaf-ud-daula, the chief minister whom the maulvi's men had taken hostage, hoping perhaps to bargain his way out with the British, or perhaps settle an old score. The minister tried to buy his release, offering Rs 2 lakh, but this was not accepted, the maulvi again accusing him of sympathy with the British. Sharaf-ud-daula was killed by Lugard's men, while the maulvi escaped, or was allowed to escape.[6]

Dargah Hazrat Abbas, 1976. Author's collection.

Between 7,000 and 8,000 supporters of the begam had fled with her and her son to Musabagh, a villa three miles west of Lucknow. At 6 a.m. on 19 March after driving out rebel sepoys from a large house belonging to a former chief minister, Ali Naqi Khan, Outram occupied Musabagh after fierce fighting and with this went the last hope of reviving an independent Awadh.

Final figures: 16 British officers, 3 native officers, 108 men killed, 595 wounded, 13 men missing.

Conclusion

There were two reasons for the Indian defeat on the battlefield of Lucknow, one of which has already been identified—lack of leadership. There was no overall command structure and no commander-in-chief. The rebel sepoys, used to following orders from their British officers, now had to rely on their own officers, the majority of whom bore only the rank of captain with a captain's experience. Protocol meant that the military junta could not command the private armies of the taluqdars but had to rely on the landowners themselves to direct their own men. Used to fighting off revenue collectors, they did not have the skills to fight off a professional, well-trained army.

There were irreconcilable disputes between the Indian leaders—the begam, the maulvi, the chief minister and, to a lesser extent, the daroga, Mammu Khan. Consequently, their followers were at war with each other too, the maulvi's Delhi Force pitted against the begam's Oudh Force, when all should have been subservient to the Sultanat-i-Birjisi, the government headed by the teenager Birjis Qadr. Neither the begam nor the chief minister had any particular loyalty or affection for the real king, Wajid Ali Shah, now imprisoned in Fort William, Calcutta. He had divorced Hazrat Mahal nearly a decade earlier and had exiled Sharaf-ud-daula from court after falling out with him.

Secondly, the Indian opposition simply did not have enough powerful artillery to counteract that of their enemy. The largest Indian cannon was no match for the 68-pounders that the British were using. Sheer weight of numbers could not compensate for inadequate artillery, as the November 1857 massacre in Sikanderbagh showed.

The role of the townspeople of Lucknow has not been adequately considered. Both sides have sought to present a picture of the entire population as either *for* them (the Indian view), or *against* them (the British view). This was simply not true. Lucknow citizens suffered grievously during the Uprising, some of it caused by Company Forces, but much of it their own fellow countrymen, who looted their shops and houses, dug up their gardens searching for treasure, repaid old grudges by accusing them of collaborating with the enemy and taxed them outrageously to pay for the sepoys' wages. Both the contemporary reporter, Kamal-ud-din Haider and a later historian writing in the 1920s, Abdul Halim Sharar, use the term *badmash* (ruffian) to describe Indian civilians who took advantage of the disturbances for their own profit.

The rebel sepoys themselves were simply doing their job, and getting paid for it, while some among them were looting where they could to supplement their meagre salaries. The idea of armed peasants rallying to the cause and flooding into Lucknow is a convenient myth. Much more convincing is the description of a huge crowd of local spectators at the Daulat Khana watching the fighting on the north bank of the river with the curiosity of an unsophisticated audience. The Uprising is the stuff of legend still, for both Indians and Britons. This short account has sought to bring some objectivity to bear on the events that happened in Lucknow between 1857 and 1858.

Practical Information for Visitors

Lucknow: The city is easily reached by air, arriving at the international Chaudhary Charan Singh Airport (formerly Amausi Airport), or by express train arriving at Charbagh Railway Station. Agra is only a four-hour drive from Lucknow.

Hotels: There are a number of good hotels, among them the long-established Taj Mahal Lucknow and the newer Lebua Lucknow Hotel based in a delightful 1930s traditional bungalow with a large garden. Clarks Awadh is an old-established well-situated hotel. All good hotels are located in Gomti Nagar while a few central hotels are found along Hazratganj.

Transport: Taxis are elusive but all hotels can order cars for guests. The simplest form of transport is the cyclerickshaw, a carriage attached to a bicycle, which can seat two people. This has the advantage of being cheap, and provides a better view because the passengers are seated higher than in a car.

Sightseeing: The Uttar Pradesh Department of Tourism is keen to attract visitors and many of the important sites associated with the Great Uprising have recently been renovated. These are all in 'new' Lucknow, the area established after 1775, although the old city is worth visiting too, especially a walk along the Chowk.

Alambagh Palace: Partially ruined, with its gatehouse now separated from the main building, this is where General James Outram fought off repeated opposition attacks during the winter of 1857/58.

No entrance fee. Adjoining it is the tomb and handsome obelisk memorial of General Sir Henry Havelock, standing in a railed enclosure and protected by the Archaeological Survey of India (ASI).

Gateway to Alambagh today. Anil Mehrotra.

Badshahbagh: Now part of the campus of the University of Lucknow, this is where Outram positioned his heavy guns to fire at the Qaisarbagh Palace, directly across the river. A neglected summer house and a small canal can still be seen here.

Bara (Great) Imambara: It remains a centre of pilgrimage for Shi'as today and an active place of worship, so shoes must be left outside and modest dress worn. Looted by the British during the recapture of the city.

Chattar Manzil and Farhat Bakhsh Palaces: They were recaptured by the British in September 1857 and provided a 'corridor' two months later when the evacuees from the Residency passed through on their way to Sikanderbagh, Dilkusha and safety. Currently being restored by the Uttar Pradesh State Archaeology Department.

Chattar Manzil, c. 2010.

Dilkusha Kothi: Now in ruins, apart from the adjoining stable block, but worth a visit. Headquarters of Sir Colin Campbell during the first relief and the recapture of the city in March 1858.

Khurshid Manzil: The Mess House of the 32nd Regiment, it is now the Martinière Girls' College, so an appointment to visit must be made through the principal. Notice the original defensive moat and

Ruins of Dilkusha today.
Anil Mehrotra.

drawbridge, which made the building particularly attractive to the regiment's officers. Subsequently used by the military junta.

The Martinière College (Boys): A spectacular building with the grave of Brigadier William Hodson in its grounds. The only school to be awarded Battle Honours for the part its pupils and staff played during the siege of the Residency. A plaque to the boys is in the central octagonal hall. This is a working school, so permission to visit must be obtained in advance from the principal.

Musabagh: Also known as Barowen, it is a car journey away. The last stand of Begam Hazrat Mahal after her flight from Qaisarbagh. Mainly ruins, but with an interesting sunken courtyard.

The Residency: An extensive site on a low hill overlooking the river Gomti, this is a protected monument under the Archaeological Survey of India. Allow a couple of hours to explore it properly. Purchase your tickets and walk in through the Baillie Guard gate that held the besiegers at bay. After this, you are on your own unless you have booked a guide through a tour operator in advance. There are

The Residency today. Anil Mehrotra.

no guidebooks, no postcards and nothing to eat or drink so take your own samosas and a plan of the buildings. There is a museum in the front portion of the Residency with a large model of the whole site. Sir Henry Lawrence is buried in the graveyard there, and there are the remains of the church where foodgrains were stored during the siege.

Rumi Darwaza: Adjacent to the Bara Imambara, the Darwaza formed one side of a large square surrounded by buildings, not dissimilar to the Registan at Samarkand. The gateway opposite Rumi Darwaza was later demolished and traffic hurtles today through what was once a sacred space.

Rumi Darwaza from the Bara Imambara. Anil Mehrotra.

Neill Darwaza: A single-arched gateway still standing where Brigadier-General James Neill was shot and killed on 25 September 1857.

Qaisarbagh: The 'citadel' and seat of government of the opposition between June 1857 and March 1858. Heavily looted by British and Nepalese forces after its recapture in March 1858 when gallows were erected in its gardens. Walk through it, avoiding the traffic. Entrance to the central barahdari, a favourite wedding venue, is free.

Shah Najaf: A place of worship with a spectacular central hall. Next to it is the Qadam-i-Rasool, an artificial hillock which once held a reputed footprint of the Prophet and was used by the British as a gunpowder store.

Sibtainabad Imambara: Located in Hazratganj, it houses the tomb of Nawab Amjad Ali Shah within a large courtyard. One of the key buildings standing between the now demolished Begam Kothi and the Qaisarbagh Palace, it was captured by Brasyer's Sikhs on 14 March 1858. Open to the public.

Sikanderbagh: The garden house which stood in the centre has gone, but a fine gateway remains and some of the walls. Entrance is by special arrangement; contact a tour operator.

Tarawali Kothi (the old observatory): It is today the main branch of the State Bank of India. Only the counter area is open to the public. This was the headquarters of Maulvi Ahmadullah Shah during the siege.

Tour Operator: Tornos is an old-established company based in Lucknow, which has been operating for over twenty-five years. Tornos conducts Mutiny tours and can suggest itineraries for visitors whose time is limited. They can book hotels and cars, and also supply knowledgeable guides. www.tornosindia.com

Notes

1. See: India Political Consultations, 10 November 1857, No. 57, India Office Records, British Library; Rosie Llewellyn-Jones, *The Great Uprising in India*, Boydell & Brewer, 2007, pp 115-16, for the text of the king's letter.

   See: Private Papers Eur. Mss, F231 22 March 1856 and 23 March 1856, India Office Records, British Library; Lord Canning, viceroy to Robert Vernon Smith, President of the Board of Control for comments on the royal party's departure from Lucknow; Rosie Llewellyn-Jones, *The Last King in India: Wajid Ali Shah*, Hurst Publishers, 2014, pp 17-18.

2. See: Nusrat Naheed, *Jane Alam aur Mehakpari*, trans. Dr J. Bhatti, Amir-ud-daula Public Library, Lucknow, 2005, p.63. 'Register of Mafi or Rent-free holdings ... District of Lucknow No. 193'. Gives details of the Begam's parents, and the grant of land by Wajid Ali Shah to her father 'Umber' in 1840.

3. See: Kamal-ud-din Haider, *Qaisar-ut-Tawarikh*, trans. Dr Hamid Afaq Qureshi, New Royal Book Company, 2008, pp 111-12, 'Entry into Qaisar Bagh and Fleeing of Janab-i'Aaliya [Begam Hazrat Mahal] on 16 March 1858. The Begam was last seen in public on 25 February 1858 when she went to Alambagh to watch the final, failed assault by the Oude Force.

4. From the Royal Collection Trust, Windsor Castle website: www.rct.uk catalogue number RCIN 1005035 - the *Isqhnama*

   'Soldiers took the manuscript and gave it to Sir John Lawrence (later Governor-General and Viceroy of India) who presented it to Queen Victoria in 1859. In a letter, Sir John Lawrence noted,

"This book is curious and interesting from two circumstances. It was prepared in the Palace of Lucknow under the direction of the King of Oude, and is of course a faithful illustration of the life and dress of the highest Mahomedan families in India. Secondly, it was taken by some Seikhs [Sikhs] of one of the Punjabee Regiments at the time the Palace of Lucknow was stormed— they gave it to their commanding officer, who was good enough to present it to me, as the Corps was raised under my orders..."'

5.   William Leslie Low, 'Lieutenant-Colonel Gould Hunter-Weston of Hunterston ... one of the defenders of Lucknow ... 1857-8. A biographical sketch', *The Scottish Chronicle*, Selkirk, 1914, p.xi

'... on the capture of the city in March 1858, his [Ahmad Ali Khan's] house was one of those from which aided by a detachment of the 20th (now the Lancashire Fusiliers), I cleared out some of the rebels. My loot consisted of two small cases containing negatives, and a bundle of hastily collected photographs, which unhappily, turned out to be failures.'

From the handwritten, unpublished notebook, p.66, of Colonel Gould Weston at Hunterston House, Ayrshire, Scotland

'It was in the mosque that after the capture of the Imambara I picked up amongst very many valuable manuscripts the two valuable Korans now in the library.' [These were subsequently sold in the 1990s.]

See: Rosie Llewellyn-Jones, 'Indian Treasures in a Scottish Country House', *Orientations*, Nov/Dec 2020, Vol. 51, No. 6.

6.   See: Kamal-ud-din Haider, *Qaisar-ut-Tawarikh*, trans. Dr Hamid Afaq Qureshi, New Royal Book Company, 2008, pp 130-31. Sharaf-ud-daula was captured by rebel sepoys and taken to the Dargah Hazrat Abbas. There, Maulvi Ahmadullah Shah demanded Rs 1 lakh from him. The minister offered Rs 2 lakh to be freed and to have someone accompany him from the dargah. This was refused and when the dargah was stormed by the British on 18th March, he was killed.

Bibliography

Barthorp, Michael, and Douglas Anderson. *The British Troops in the Indian Mutiny 1857–59.* Osprey Publishing Ltd, 1994.

Forbes-Mitchell, William. *Reminiscences of the Great Mutiny 1857–59.* London: Macmillan & Co., 1910.

Forrest, G.W. *A History of the Indian Mutiny. Reviewed and Illustrated from Original Documents.* Vol. 2. Edinburgh & London: William Blackwood & Sons, 1904.

Gubbins, Martin. *An Account of the Mutinies in Oudh and of the Siege of the Lucknow Residency.* 3rd ed. London: Richard Bentley, 1858.

Haider, Kamal-ud-din. *Qaisar-ul-tawareekh: Tareekh Awadh.* Lucknow: Nawal Kishore, 1879.

Llewellyn-Jones, Rosie. *The Great Uprising in India, 1857–58: Untold Stories, Indian and British.* The Boydell Press, 2007.

Llewellyn-Jones, Rosie. 'Africans in the Indian Mutiny', *History Today.* Vol. 59, Issue 12, December 2009.

Llewellyn-Jones, Rosie. *The Last King in India: Wajid Ali Shah.* London: Hurst Publishing, 2014.

Llewellyn-Jones, Rosie, ed. *The Uprising of 1857.* Ahmedabad: Mapin Publishing Ltd with the Alkazi Collection of Photography, Delhi, 2017.

Mukherjee, Rudrangshu. *Awadh in Revolt 1857–1858: A Study of Popular Resistance.* Delhi: Permanent Black, 2002.

Roberts, Frederick. *Forty-one Years in India: From Subaltern to Commander-in-Chief.* Vol. 1, London: Richard Bentley & Son, 1897.

Russell, William. *My Diary in India, in the Year 1858–9.* London: Routledge, Warne & Routledge, 1869.

Taqui, Roshan. *Lucknow 1857 (The Two Wars at Lucknow: The Dusk of an Era).* Lucknow: New Royal Book Co., 2001.

Taqui, Roshan, ed. *Images of Lucknow.* Lucknow: New Royal Book Co., 2005.

Taylor, P.J.O. *A Companion to the 'Indian Mutiny' of 1857.* Delhi: Oxford University Press, 1996.

Taylor, P.J.O. *What Really Happened During the Mutiny: A Day-by-Day Account of the Major Events of 1857–1858 in India.* Delhi: Oxford University Press, 1997.

[Wilson, Major T.F.]. *The Defence of Lucknow: A Diary … from 31st May to 25th September 1857.* 'By a Staff Officer'. London: Smith, Elder & Co., 1858.

Index

Acknowledgements

MY THANKS ARE DUE FIRSTLY to Squadron Leader Rana T.S. Chhina MBE (Retd), former Vice President of the now defunct Indian Military Historical Society, who invited me to write this book, and to the United Service Institution of India Centre for Military History and Conflict Studies for initiating the series.

To Brigadier Bill Woodburn, who kindly spent a day familiarizing me with military terminology of the mid-nineteenth century.

To Derek Johnson, an old Martinian, Lucknow, who kindly sent me a handsome selection of maps and plans of the city which have proved invaluable in tracing the buildings within the Residency compound.

To Roshan Taqui, the Lucknow-based historian who read the first draft of this book and suggested helpful amendments.

To Colonel Anil Mehrotra and Dr Tulika Sahu for providing photographs of the sites today.

To Sir Mark Havelock-Allan Bt QC, for the map by Captain F.H.M. Sitwell.

To Andrew Ward, my fellow author, for the 'Plan of Lucknow' map of 1857-58.

Of all the horrors that blackened the uprising of 1857, none could match the atrocities committed at Kanpur.

In *Kanpur, 1857*—part of a new series of books on India's historic battles—historian Andrew Ward gives an unblinking account of the siege of the entrenchment into which the European community fled when the town's four native regiments rebelled, the massacre at the Sati Chaura Ghat, and the hacking to death of the surviving Europeans. Their slaughter would exacerbate the savage and indiscriminate killings the British were already carrying out, burning villages and condemning thousands of locals to flogging, degradation and the gallows.

This richly illustrated field guide draws on decades of research to depict the pitched battles, and the acts of heroism and sacrifice on both sides that were subsumed by campaigns of atrocity and terror.

About the United Service
Institution of India

ESTABLISHED IN 1870 BY MAJOR General Sir Charles MacGregor in Shimla (then Simla), the United Service Institution of India (USI) is a national security and defence services think tank based in New Delhi. Its aim is the 'furtherance of interest and knowledge in the art, science and literature of the defence services'. It is located at Vasant Vihar, New Delhi, from where it has been operating since 1996.

About the Centre for Military History and Conflict Studies (Formerly Centre for Armed Forces Historical Research)

THE CENTRE WAS ESTABLISHED IN December 2000 under the aegis of the USI for encouraging the objective study of all facets of Indian military history with a special emphasis on the history of the Indian Armed Forces. It focuses on diverse aspects of the history of Indian military evolution, policies and practices—strategic, tactical, logistical, organisational and socio-economic, as well as the field of contemporary conflict studies.

About the Author

Dr Rosie Llewellyn-Jones, MBE, studied Urdu and Hindi at the School of Oriental and African Studies. She was awarded a first-class honours degree and completed her PhD there, which was subsequently published as *A Fatal Friendship: The Nawabs, the British and the City of Lucknow* in 1985. She visits the subcontinent as frequently as possible and was an invited speaker at a recent Jaipur Literature Festival. She has been the archivist at the Royal Society for Asian Affairs for ten years and a Council Member of the Royal Asiatic Society. She was awarded an MBE in 2015 for services to the British Association for Cemeteries in South Asia (BACSA) and British Indian studies.

The aftermath of an exploded mine under the Chattar Manzil.

PBD
10 3/5/73